D1481430

FINITE CAPACITY
SCHEDULING

Oliver Wight
Manufacturing Series

FINITE CAPACITY SCHEDULING

Management, Selection, and Implementation

Gerhard Plenert
Bill Kirchmier

JOHN WILEY & SONS, INC.
New York • Chichester • Weinheim • Brisbane • Singapore • Toronto

Library of Congress Cataloging-in-Publication Data:
Plenert, Gerhard Johannes.
    Finite capacity scheduling : management, selection, and implementation / Gerhard Plenert, Bill Kirchmier.
      p.   cm.—(Oliver Wight manufacturing series)
    Includes index.
    ISBN 0-471-35264-0 (cloth : alk. paper)
    1. Production scheduling. I. Kirchmier, Bill, 1931– II. Title. III. Series.
TS157.5.P58 2000
658.5′3—dc21   99-044971

I dedicate this book to the understanding that the true purpose of life is in learning how to give, not how to get—and in learning that giving has eternal rewards attached to it.

I also dedicate this book to my wife, Renee Sangray Plenert, who never ceases to amaze me.

—G.P.

I dedicate this book to my ex-wife, Dessa Brashear. The book would not have been written without her continued efforts to convince me that the information should be published. Through Dessa's persuasion plus her actual contributions to the text, as well as her attending my seminars to become more familiar with the subject, formatting a preliminary outline, and several years of support, the book had its beginning.

Dessa's efforts were responsible for motivating me to embark on the project. I am deeply grateful.

—B.K.

Contents

CONTENTS

Acknowledgments

In order to give credit where credit is due I would have to go back to the earliest days of my work experience when I worked in a variety of small to medium-sized plants in Oregon. Later I worked for NCR Corporation in the international manufacturing division, and for Clark Equipment Company in plants as far away as Indonesia, Australia, Chile, and Germany, and as close as Ohio and Mexico. My broad exposure to a variety of manufacturing facilities all over the world has provided the background I needed to write this book.

I also need to recognize my family—my wife, Renee Sangray Plenert, and my children, Heidi Lynette Plenert, Dawn Janelle Plenert, Gregory Johannes Plenert, Gerick Johannes Plenert, Joshua Johannes Plenert, Natasha Ida Plenert, Zackary Johannes Plenert, and Chelsey Jean Plenert, who gave me the time I needed to make this book work.

—G.P.

Like all books, contributions for this one come from many sources; only a few will be noted. First is Paul Wyman, who was the primary influence in my involvement in the Finite Capacity Scheduling (FCS) industry. Paul was a pioneer in the FCS industry as founder and president of JobTime Systems, Inc., since 1983. I worked as a partner with Paul for 10 years and he has been a significant influence in my education on the subject. The book certainly would not exist if Paul had not been instrumental in my joining JobTime Systems.

Ken Cybulsky at McDermott International was the second individual to have a major influence. Ken's observations and classification of scheduling methods added a new dimension to my seminars and set the stage for this book. I continued to learn from Ken during the installation of several FCS systems at McDermott International.

Working with early innovators at many companies, too numerous to mention, added insights into how and how not to implement FCS. Many of these early innovators risked their positions by committing to implement FCS before it had become a respectable technology.

—B.K.

About the Authors

GERHARD PLENERT

Gerhard Plenert, PhD, CPIM, has spent 20 years working in management for private industry. His specialty is in international POM (production/operations management) and MIS (management information systems). He has traveled throughout the world in this capacity. He returned to school to earn his PhD at the Colorado School of Mines. He spent four years teaching and doing research at California State University, Chico, and eight years at Brigham Young University in the Institute of Business Management. He was the director of the California Productivity and Quality Center at CSUC and the director of the Productivity and Quality Research Group at BYU. He has recently returned to industry and in an attempt to demonstrate that the topics covered in this book really do work he successfully accomplished the following in eight months:

Drove a 14+ percent defect rate down to below 2 percent.

Brought setup times from over 20 minutes to as low as 6 minutes.

Established QS (Quality Systems) certification, TQM (Total Quality Management), and SPC (Statistical Process Control), and recertified under ISO (International Standards Organization).

Performed world-class manufacturing. MRP II (Manufacturing Resources Planning), and ERP (Enterprise Resources Planning) training.

Organized a research and development (R&D) department.

Reduced inventories by 40 percent.

Significantly reduced the overall lead time and cycle time.

Reduced order preparation time from five days to less than one day.

Organized the development of corporate and departmental vision, mission, and values statements and a strategy.

Organized a previously nonexistent production planning and scheduling function, which focuses on Finite Capacity Scheduling using an MRP II base.

His research specialty is in international industrial management with an emphasis on developing countries. He has published over 130 articles, and has made over 150 conference and seminar presentations. He has published four books:

International Management and Production: Survival Techniques for Corporate America, Blue Ridge Summit, PA: Tab Professional and Reference Books, 1990.

Plant Operations Deskbook, Homewood, IL: Business 1 Irwin, 1993.

World Class Manager, Rocklin, CA: Prima Publishing, 1995.

Making Innovation Happen: Concept Management through Integration (with Shozo Hibino), Boca Raton, FL: St. Lucie Press, 1997.

Mr. Plenert realizes that the subject matter of this book is very fluid and dynamic. He is very interested in your experiences, comments, ideas, and recommendations and would find them helpful in further editions of this book. Please send your comments to him at:

Gerhard Plenert, PhD, CPIM
Senior Principal, American Management Systems (AMS)
8545 Sunset Ave., Fair Oaks, CA 95628
plenert@aol.com
Phone 916-536-9751, fax 916-536-9758

BILL KIRCHMIER

Bill Kirchmier has a long and varied career in multiple industries. Forty years have passed since his becoming a mechanical engineer. The first five years involved technical sales and application of heavy industrial equipment, including diesel engines, pumps, and compressors, at Fairbanks Morse & Co. in the Pacific Northwest and British Columbia. The next five years were spent at the Rucker Company working in design and implementation of hydraulic and pneumatic control systems in a broad range of industries that were mostly manufacturing-related. Bill's time at Fairbanks Morse and the Rucker Company contributed important experience in manufacturing.

He joined GE Timesharing in 1968 and has remained in some segment of the computer industry since then. He spent a productive and valuable 10 years at Optimum Systems Inc., as manager of sales and technical support in the San Francisco office. OSI was a pioneer in the computer services industry, supplying remote batch computer services on IBM mainframes and application software. Bill established software applications for project management, structural design, and linear programming that accounted for a large portion of the total company business.

Each of the previous experiences contributed to some aspect of the book; however, the most meaningful experience was as a partner and member of the Finite Capacity Scheduling (FCS) development and implementation team at JobTime Systems. During this 10-year period he installed or modeled over 200 FCS applications in a broad range of industries throughout the world. The applications varied from production of nuclear fuel to fiber optics and from book publishing to offshore oil well drilling rigs and remanufacturing applications.

He determined that the education of prospective customers was a prerequisite to selling FCS systems in those early days and developed a training program titled "Understanding, Selecting and Implementing FCS." The program has educated hundreds of management and shop floor personnel about finite scheduling.

He left JobTime Systems in January 1996, and continues to expand the seminar program to assist prospective FCS users in selecting and implementing FCS systems.

Preface

If every factory in the world worked in exactly the same way, this book would have been very easy to write. Unfortunately, our experience is that no two factories work alike. Even when the factories are producing the same product and are right next to each other, they often operate differently because of management style and influence, or corporate influences. Therefore, it is difficult to come up with one book and then to claim that this is the perfect way to run all international facilities. That is why we will not make that claim. One might apply Newton's law to manufacturing: *"For every expert with a perfect solution there is an equal and opposite expert with a perfect solution."*

The purpose of this book is to take manufacturing scheduling methodology into the future. In the past, techniques like Economic Order Quantity (EOQ) and Material Requirements Planning (MRP) were the buzzwords of manufacturing planning excellence. These have been updated by Manufacturing Resources Planning (MRP II), Just-in-Time (JIT), Enterprise Resource Planning (ERP), and Theory of Constraints (TOC), which have refocused the planning process and have more closely aligned it with world-class manufacturing needs. With these systems, quality and productivity were the measures of competitive success. However, the future requires us to focus also on time. A futuristic competitive stance requires that we stay on the alert for techniques that will shorten cycle time, manage the supply chain, reduce costs, and increase responsiveness to customer requirements. Finite Capacity Scheduling (FCS) has become this tool of the future, and the purpose of this book is to demonstrate how FCS will take current manufacturing processes into a time-focused future.

This book's discussion of FCS will expose the inherent problems associated with infinite capacity scheduling and point out the management changes required to move from infinite capacity to Finite Capacity Scheduling (FCS). This book will influence management to move to FCS methods and to think in terms of time-based production, not just a material-based production.

This book will demonstrate:

➤ The production improvement potential available with FCS scheduling.

➤ How to be time-based and schedule for short cycle times and predictable due dates.

This book will take the futuristic step of overcoming the inertia of the long-term use of infinite capacity backward pass (ICBP) scheduling methods and replace them with FCS. This will require in-depth management changes. The traditional infinite capacity scheduling method used by MRP and MRP II systems are self-defeating, yield unfeasible results, and waste resources, not only shop floor resources but resources throughout the organization.

The acceptance and long-term use of an infinite capacity scheduling method is so deeply entrenched that a significant amount of education will be required to move personnel and management to a more sophisticated and functional scheduling method. The resistance of MRP vendors, until recently, to adopt the use of Finite Capacity Scheduling (FCS) has been yet another cause for the continued use of infinite capacity scheduling. This book will address the issues behind this resistance to accepting FCS and logically point out why there is an urgent need to move rapidly toward methods that produce feasible solutions for both MRP and ERP vendors and their customers.

The book will demonstrate that feasible scheduling and time-based measurements are core factors for being able to efficiently to implement significant production improvements. Change management concepts play a major role in the transition and it should be noted that tools like Total Quality Management (TQM), Process Reengineering (PR), and others add support to this direction.

Many companies are promoting themselves as having reached world-class manufacturing status. Most of these companies are still using infinite capacity scheduling. Is it realistic to strive for world-class status while operating under unfeasible schedules?

The definition of insanity is continuing to do the same things and expecting different results.

— *Breakthrough Thinking*, NADLER and HIBINO[1]

---

[1]Gerald Nadler and Shozo Hibino, *Breakthrough Thinking*, Rocklin, CA: Prima Pub., 1989.

Introduction

What is more important than managing your resources?

Volumes have been written about Material Requirements Planning (MRP), Just-in-Time (JIT), cells, and other such methods to improve productivity in the manufacturing environment. The current new hot topics are Enterprise Resource Planning (ERP), Supply Chain Management (SCM), Theory of Constraints (TOC), and others. While all of these techniques offer potential improvement, none adequately addresses the problem of scheduling. Most MRP vendors continue to offer infinite capacity scheduling solutions. Software vendors often use the term FCS (Finite Capacity Scheduling) to describe their systems; however, the term FCS is so loosely used that its meaning has become vague. This book will help to clear up the confusion about what FCS really is and how it can be used to improve the scheduling process.

There is a new paradigm that states that accurate scheduling is here. However, the old MRP paradigm (infinite capacity) has been in place for so long that personnel trained in traditional scheduling techniques are having a difficult time progressing to the new level. This long-term position has created a condition of severe static inertia. Human inertia is predominately a positive element of human character. It tends to keep things in a definitive direction. However, when a paradigm shift occurs and the potential for a quantum leap is on the horizon, this same inertia gets in the way of progress. Traditional training in the use of infinite capacity fits the old paradigm.

For the past 15 years, the authors have been involved with installing and/or modeling more than 200 FCS scheduling applications. In the process of promoting FCS systems, we realized very early that the real problem inhibiting better scheduling has been the lack of education about modern techniques and the near universal acceptance of infinite scheduling. The overwhelming promotion of infinite capacity backward pass scheduling for so many years has created a de facto acceptance attitude.

We have concluded that no one, including management, really expects traditional scheduling systems to produce results accurate enough to be followed on the shop floor. In most production facilities, the department manager or shop foreman is the person who ultimately determines the actual sequence of events. Lots of discussion takes place in most companies about planning and scheduling. Production meetings are held and most often the end result is that the hot jobs get expedited. This has been the ultimate cure for inadequate scheduling.

Our solution to overcome this scenario was to create a book and seminar designed to educate participants in alternate and modern scheduling methods. The seminar evolved over the years and much of the content of this book is based on information gained from participants over the time that these seminars have been conducted. The experience gained in actual implementations of FCS scheduling systems has obviously also contributed to this book's contents.

There is nothing permanent except change.
—Heraclitus, Greek philosopher

Part I

HISTORY OF
MANUFACTURING SCHEDULING

Chapter 1

Why Schedule?

*Behold the turtle. He only makes progress
when he sticks his neck out.*
—JAMES B. CONANT

INTRODUCTION

Do you remember the slide rule? For those of you who don't, let me describe it to you. A slide rule is made up of three sticks; the two outer sticks are connected together and the center stick slides back and forth between them. There are gradient marks on all three sticks and these marks form a logarithmic scale that is used for calculations like multiplication and division. Ten years ago, understanding and using the slide rule was still part of the mandatory training in the engineering schools of most universities. Now slide rules are considered to be antiques. Why? Because they can no longer calculate? Or, because they give the wrong answer? No! The reason the slide rule has become obsolete is because a newer, faster, and more accurate tool has been developed: the electronic calculator. Today, someone who still uses a slide rule would be considered to be a fool. A better tool exists, so why not use it?

The same is true in the use of scheduling systems. First there was the two-bin system. Next came Economic Order Quantity (EOQ). With the advent of the computer, Material Requirements Planning (MRP) became possible. And then there were additional scheduling improvements like Just-in-Time (JIT) and Theory of Constraints (TOC). With each new wave of technology came the obsolescence of the older technology. Today, running a production facility based strictly on EOQ modeling would be considered seriously outdated. We are now ready for the next wave of technology. This book will introduce the reader to the scheduling methodology for the year 2000 and beyond: Finite Capacity Scheduling (FCS).

The appearance of Finite Capacity Scheduling (FCS) systems in the early 1980s created heated and extended debates about the value of traditional MRP infinite scheduling methods versus the newer finite scheduling methods. The resistance to finite scheduling was particularly high among MRP vendors and long-term MRP users. The introduction of FCS represented a paradigm shift, and paradigm shifts upset the status quo.

WHY SWITCH?

Planning cycle time has been reduced from two days per line to just four hours for all lines. This allows us to integrate the company's manufacturing lines and supply

chain with assurance that a balanced
schedule will secure our industry-leading
quality standard.
—JAMES SYPNIEWSKI, manager,
business analysis, Volvo Trucks NA[1]

Headquartered in Greensboro, North Carolina, Volvo
Trucks North America has approximately half a million
trucks on the roads of North America. Volvo manages its
production process through I2 Technologies' RHYTHM[®][2]
FCS system utilizing 70 to 80 constraints. It adds and sub-
tracts constraints as needed. Integrating this with material
requirements generates a single schedule for all Volvo facilities and, following the supply chain, down to its vendors.
Volvo has the flexibility to schedule truck model production
while respecting capacity constraints and maintaining efficient flow.

The biggest benefit we have seen is an
improved ability to respond to customer
requests. If we can respond quickly in our
scheduling, we can get that information out
to our supply base so that they can respond
quickly too.
—JAMES SYPNIEWSKI, manager,
business analysis, Volvo Trucks NA[3]

[1]Taken from an article on Volvo Trucks NA in the February 1997 issue of *Manufacturing Systems* and from an I2 customer case study sheet.
[2]RHYTHM is a registered trademark of I2 Technologies, Inc. I2 Technologies is
headquartered in Irving, Texas.
[3]From *Manufacturing Systems*, February 1997, and I2 customer case study
sheet.

The question "Why switch?" for traditional scheduling devotees has drawn firm firing lines. The traditionalists believed that the slide rule did an adequate job and that the new technology was not necessary. Even in the mid-1990s, most members of the American Production and Inventory Control Society (APICS) manufacturing information database (MFG-INFO) unequivocally expressed this same attitude when the list requested responses from members regarding the virtues of infinite and finite scheduling.

Infinite capacity scheduling has been strongly endorsed by the MRP community for the past 25 years and any suggestion of an improvement was treated as heresy. In the late 1990s attitudes had changed and MRP vendors started offering FCS solutions. The question shifted away from "Why switch?" to "What to switch to?" Potential users were interested in learning which vendor system would be the long-term winner and would remain at the forefront of FCS technology.

International competitive pressures "to be considered the best" slowly forced users to reconsider their selection of a scheduling technique. The change was inevitable; FCS works. It has always been self-evident that making illogical assumptions, like assuming that a factory had an infinite amount of capacity, would yield illogical answers. A better solution exists when logical assumptions are made. The reason behind the strong resistance was that both the MRP vendors and the long-term users would be required to make significant changes. Additionally, there would be large financial commitments for the MRP vendors in a change of this type. These were not comfortable conditions, and it took some time to convince vendors and users of the value behind the change.

The August 1998 issue of *APICS—The Performance Ad-*

vantage published Bill Kirchmier's article entitled "Selecting an Application: Finite Capacity Scheduling Methods." An excerpt of the article follows (the full article can be found in Appendix 1.1):

> The question regarding finite capacity scheduling (FCS) is not so much "Is my company ready for FCS?" but "Can we afford to wait?" Companies that have implemented FCS systems and made the necessary cultural changes have reaped productivity improvements and realized competitive advantages.
>
> I'd like to begin by quoting Laura D'Andrea Tyson, dean of the Haas School of Business at the University of California at Berkeley and previous economic advisor to President Clinton, who said: "Productivity growth is the key variable not only in the trade-off between inflation and unemployment, but also in the economy's long-run growth performance. Over time, output growth is determined by the improvement in productivity."
>
> Improved productivity through better utilization of resources is what finite capacity scheduling is all about.
>
> FCS systems have evolved and matured over the past 10 years, and more than 100 packaged software alternatives are now commercially available. The capabilities and costs of these systems vary dramatically, with no single system reigning supreme. With the growth and success in the number of FCS systems, plus a continuing increase in installations by early adapters, many companies today use such scheduling methods.
>
> But the emergence of FCS systems has created tension in the ranks of devoted MRP/MRP II/ERP users, with heated debates swirling about the value of FCS. In reality, however, there should be no conflict. MRP systems solve material and, to some degree planning problems, whereas FCS systems solve only scheduling problems.

Minus the perceived conflict, MRP/ERP systems and FCS systems are truly natural partners.

To appreciate the value of FCS systems, one should realize that moving from traditional scheduling techniques to any FCS system would improve productivity, if appropriate cultural changes were implemented. Two of the major motivating factors for moving from traditional scheduling to FCS scheduling are the universal demand for short cycle times and predictability of delivery dates.

Many companies perceive the discipline required for implementing and maintaining FCS systems as being too great to justify moving to FCS. Ultimately, however, the commitment must be made. The increased success of companies that make the move will put pressure on competitive companies that stick with traditional scheduling.

TYPES OF FCS METHODS

There are three major categories of FCS scheduling methodologies. These are:

➤ Job-based.

➤ Resource-based.

➤ Event-based.

Future chapters will discuss these in detail. Additionally, there are methodologies that carry the FCS banner and therefore deserve mention. However, these have only a limited number of installations. For example, genetic algorithm and linear programming are the most notable. Some FCS vendors also refer to heuristics as another method. However, since some, if not all, of the job-based, resource-based, and event-based systems use heuristics as a technique within their primary approach, it is difficult to consider this an alternative method.

With a variety of methods and many vendors to choose from, it is little surprise that traditional MRP advocates are concerned about the future direction of scheduling technology. Part of the confusion stems from a lack of clear distinctions between planning systems and scheduling systems.

Planning versus Scheduling

Material Requirements Planning (MRP) systems claim to have both planning and scheduling. However, with today's finite scheduling advances, MRP with its infinite capacity backward pass approach is not capable of producing a schedule that could be followed on the shop floor. Infinite scheduling was used for many years by MRP systems with limited results. Its long-term use has created a feeling that infinite scheduling is an acceptable and effective scheduling method. In reality, the best that can be said about infinite scheduling is that it functioned as a modest planning system. A lot has recently been published about the inadequacy of infinite capacity scheduling.

Planning is the process of calculating material and capacity demands as accurately as possible based on forecast orders, actual orders, or both over a specified time. The terms forecasting and planning both imply error. The output document to the shop floor from an infinite capacity system is a dispatch list that specifies which products are to be produced and in what quantities. The document includes the due date of each work order and the sequence of events but not the time the events will take place at each work center. This document is typically used by the manager to assist in determining the sequence of tasks through each work center. This approach limits the ability to coordinate work throughout the entire plant. Infinite scheduling compares to a 30-piece band with each musician playing a different tune.

In contrast, scheduling implies accuracy. Scheduling is the process of accurately defining the operating conditions for production on a minute-by-minute basis. Unlike planning, the scheduling function covers a relatively short interval of time. Scheduling used in this context implies that any resource that will affect production needs to be accurately scheduled (i.e., machines, personnel, fixtures, tools, outside vendors, etc.). The output document from a finite scheduling system accurately defines the sequence of all tasks through each work center on a minute-by-minute basis and coordinates all work centers to improve overall plant throughput. The fact that FCS schedules are calculated to such accuracy causes concern that it may not be possible to follow this schedule on a minute-by-minute basis. True, it is not possible to precisely follow a schedule to that degree; however, if the schedule is not calculated to that degree of accuracy, errors would be imposed before it gets to the shop floor.

Actual conditions will oscillate around the FCS-generated scheduled conditions but will be within acceptable limits. When the actual conditions deviate to an unacceptable degree, an update of conditions is required and a new schedule is created. When routings are reasonably accurate and data input is reliable, following the schedule is not a problem and schedules are often followed to the end of the expected cycle without the need for interim rescheduling.

In summary, planning is a close approximation of future conditions over an extended period and scheduling is an accurate list of events based on current conditions over a short interval. Some industries may be able to continue to function and remain competitive with only a planning system and without the need for a detailed scheduling system, but they will be the exception.

THE SPECTRUM OF MANUFACTURING

A variety of processes exist in manufacturing with flow shops and job shops at opposite ends of the spectrum. Although FCS is a benefit to companies at either end of the spectrum, the benefit is more prominent toward the job shop end of the spectrum. Most companies operate somewhere between these two extremes. However, the trend is moving toward the job shop end because customer orders, lot sizes, and cycle time demands are all getting smaller. Even product areas that are traditionally flow shops are beginning to look more like job shops. To be competitive in the future, most companies will have to resort to better scheduling technology. Planning systems alone will not fill the bill.

WHY SCHEDULE?

When considering the question "Why schedule?" it is necessary to focus on three universal business success factors:

1. Quality.

2. On-time delivery.

3. Price.

Scheduling impacts the first two of these three items. American industry today is striving to improve its efficiency and effectiveness and to shorten product cycle times. Two strong fads are Total Quality Management (TQM) and Business Process Reengineering (BPR). The Holy Grail is reliable production in the shortest time. The measure of success is almost always time-based.

The first time-based measure is predictability—the ability to deliver when quoted. Thus we get the TQM mantra of "Say what you do, and do what you say." The second measure is cycle time reduction. This is the shortening of the time needed to produce an order. To accomplish these two time-based criteria requires capacity management, which requires effective scheduling. As Peter Drucker persuasively argues, the new measure of competitive success is, or should be, time. The true measure of productivity is output per unit of time given finite resources.

The time-based objective of scheduling should be to define when jobs will be completed and to deliver the jobs on that schedule; to deliver the product when promised. The cost of late delivery is high. At worst, it means lost orders or even lost customers, but it often also means excess inventory with high buffer inventories, poor customer relations, and excessive expediting. The bottom line costs are easily calculable. In contrast, the ideal schedule will:

1. Maximize resource utilization.

2. Decrease inventory costs.

3. Increase inventory turnover.

4. Improve customer service.

5. Improve communication and coordination.

6. Produce a to-do list that can be followed.

SCHEDULING STARTS WITH A STRATEGIC PLAN

A strategic plan should address conditions that promote company objectives; these objectives are modeled in the scheduling system to promote adherence to the company strategy. Some important issues, which have often been left out of a company's strategy, include:

1. Methods of quoting due dates.

2. Periodic evaluations of the strategic plan.

3. Sufficient attention to companywide communication (data accessible to all personnel when and where needed).

Failure to define and follow each of the points at all levels will tend to undermine the scheduling objectives. The end result will be a tendency to deviate from the schedule and lose its intended effectiveness.

Even the best companies tend to be reactive because of poor scheduling. Often their employees prefer being reactive because they are so used to operating in this mode. The shoot from the hip approach is very common in the American culture. The West was won with a six-shooter and many shop floor managers continue to function in the shoot from the hip mode. While there are some conditions that might benefit from this philosophy, modern, competitive, and complex manufacturing is not one of them.

Capacity Requirements Planning (CRP) as discussed in MRP systems is based on infinite capacity scheduling. However, very few companies ever implement the MRP Capacity Requirements Planning (CRP) modules because they are not effective. They cannot produce feasible schedules.

Most MRP systems issue a report to the shop floor referred to as the dispatch list. This report is simply a list of the jobs with due dates. No document is delivered to the shop floor that details when each task should be produced at each work center. Fortunately, this is starting to change. Some MRP software companies are slowly becoming aware of and taking steps to provide better scheduling. It will, however, take years before management's current expectations are met.

This book will repeatedly point to the scheduling inadequacies of MRP systems and it may appear at times that we think MRP systems are of little use. This is not the case; to set the record straight, MRP systems and next-generation Enterprise Resource Planning (ERP) systems are here to stay, and they contribute greatly to the material management function. But as a capacity management function, current MRP systems are totally inadequate and produce unfeasible results due to the assumption that capacity is infinite. This book shows how MRP systems can make a quantum leap in effectiveness by implementing Finite Capacity Scheduling (FCS) methods within the MRP structure.

Management Involvement in Scheduling Hardware and Software Systems

Scheduling is computer intensive, and until the advent of cheap computing in the 1980s computer power posed a prohibitive technical barrier. Sophisticated solutions to scheduling are fairly new. Implementation of modern scheduling systems remains rather obscure. Scheduling is a management problem, yet most often scheduling decisions are relegated to the shop floor. We suspect that most managers believe that meaningful, precise scheduling is not possible. Very few managers understand the dimensions of scheduling. Operations management is not a popular subject since it requires more technology, demands more education, and gets in the way of the traditionalist's shoot from the hip philosophy.

Newer system concepts are now entering the scene and will be discussed. These new systems tend to offer functions beyond the typical MRP systems. The most prominent new concepts now being promoted and receiving significant attention are Enterprise Resource Planning (ERP), Finite Capacity Promising (FCP), Schedule-Based Manufacturing (SBM), and Supply Chain Management (SCM). These systems deal with a broader base of information than the typical MRP systems. However, at the time of writing this book, most of the mentioned disciplines have not yet made a full commitment to modern scheduling technology.

Modern scheduling technology is now moving ahead at an impressive rate. Vendors are being faced with a continuous array of new customer demands. As new requirements are realized, vendors add features and functions. Vendor systems are beginning to converge toward similar characteristics, and this trend toward standardization will continue. As vendors win new and more clients, each vendor must ultimately match each new application to the satisfaction of clients or be eliminated from the competition. The result is that vendor systems begin to appear similar even though they use different scheduling methods.

A major objective in moving toward modern scheduling is to motivate management to get involved in the process of scheduling. Most companies seem content to accept the standard approach of infinite scheduling and to assign materials management the scheduling function. Most often the default position is to accept the traditional MRP approach without considering new and advanced methods that yield better solutions and reduce cycle times. A major function of this book is to demonstrate to management why implementation of time-based manufacturing is necessary for the coordination of material and capacity.

It will be necessary to influence a large number of high-level management personnel throughout the manufacturing sector before FCS becomes an accepted approach. This chapter will be dedicated to convincing upper-level management that infinite capacity scheduling is bankrupt and produces unfeasible schedules. The chapter will also expose the need for upper-level management to coordinate the scheduling method with the management style of the company.

We are now ready to move forward and learn what FCS is all about. How can FCS make a manufacturer more competitive? Let's find out.

MANAGEMENT STYLES

Experience in implementing FCS systems over the past 14 years has resulted in some observations. One of the most discernible and useful observations is that practically all scheduling management has been based on a style that we refer to as job management. Wherever we implemented FCS, regardless of the product being manufactured, there was a recurrence of expediting. After several years of observing excessive expediting, it occurred to us that the problem was related to the inability to predict finish dates of customer orders. Finish dates were often later than due dates or would require expediting and overtime to meet the established due date commitment.

Observing this condition led to the realization that several factors combine to create a perpetual condition of expediting. The process of piecing together the various influences on production and delivery commitments led to the conclusion that infinite capacity scheduling was the primary culprit. Infinite scheduling is not the sole contributor; the effort to satisfy clients in the absence of accurate data was also a large contributor to the chaos. Acceptance of standard cycle times also contributed.

Most companies would apply some standard delivery time (predetermined product cycle time) for each product and quote the standard regardless of the load in the shop. To further exasperate the condition, because companies like to be responsive to client needs or demands, and because of pressure from the sales department, the manufacturer would usually quote whatever delivery the client insisted on.

The next chapter will go into detail about how infinite scheduling functions; a brief explanation here will give some understanding of why infinite scheduling contributes to the problem. Infinite scheduling systems assume that a task can be started whenever it arrives at a work center. This is an incorrect assumption. In an attempt to correct this assumption, estimated queue time is added to the standard production lead time at each work center. This is time above what it would take to complete the product if infinite capacity did exist. This estimated time is based on some average and does not take into account the actual current demand; ignoring variable demand is a second incorrect assumption. Other erroneous assumptions also occur; however, the two major problems are based on the following erroneous assumptions:

➢ A task can be started whenever it arrives at a work center.

➢ The average queue time can be expected.

Often a customer is on the phone ordering a product and requesting a delivery date that is much earlier than the date calculated by the system. Since everyone is aware that the system is not accurate and that the estimated dates are much longer than the actual work content, the client gets promised the date requested. If this were the only exception to the estimated cycle time, there would be no problem because with infinite capacity systems these estimates are always conservative and much longer than normal deliveries. However, when the next customer calls with a delivery date request and also gets the delivery date desired, the problem is compounded. The result is that the exception becomes the standard and soon practically all jobs end up needing to be expedited if they are to meet the due date. This is an extremely costly way to run a manufacturing facility.

SCHEDULING METHODS

Most companies that implement software of any variety, be it accounting, forecasting, or material control, use only a portion of what the software system has to offer. They do not realize the total capability of the software. Scheduling software follows the same pattern. However, users of scheduling software utilize even less of the total capability than users of most other types of software. The permutations and combinations of features and functions, constraints, rules, user priorities, due dates, setup minimization, preferred workstations, and so on are so numerous that many users continue to resort to intuition rather than using the system's capability to find the best solution.

To utilize a modern scheduling technology requires deviating from traditional practices. For example, the constrained work centers (bottlenecks) become the major influence in limiting throughput. Regardless of what decisions are made relative to priorities, setup minimization, rules used, and so forth, the controlling factor is that bottleneck work centers have more demand than capacity. In many applications, and particularly in a job shop environment, these constraints often move from work center to work center (wandering bottlenecks).

The user's objective is to let the scheduling system find the best solution. A good approach is to generate multiple schedules using varying parameters and compare the results. This may not be optimum because it is difficult to define a truly optimum solution when so many conflicting conditions exist. Rather, this is the best solution based on current conditions.

Using an FCS system requires experience and has a learning curve prior to reaping the rewards available from modern scheduling technology, and this requires a concerted effort. Intuitive methods should remain; however, the major emphasis should focus on making use of the power of the scheduling software. Intuition resulting from years of experience should be used in conjunction with the FCS system capability to investigate options. The combination of human ingenuity and alternative schedules from the scheduling system can generate better results in only a few minutes.

The acceleration of the acceptance of FCS in the past few years has left MRP vendors vulnerable because of their resistance in accepting FCS systems. Most good FCS development has been by independent vendors who offer only scheduling software. Some MRP vendors have attempted to develop FCS systems. However, their efforts to date have not been very impressive or rewarding, and the result has forced MRP vendors to partner or purchase scheduling software from independent FCS developers, many of whom have over 10 years of development and implementation experience.

These MRP/ERP vendors feel they have fully integrated their new partner or their purchased software, and to some extent it is true. The ultimate solution and true integration of material and capacity would require starting over and building the material and capacity systems together as a single solution. This is no small task and will take years. Trying to solve all material and capacity conflicts in a single pass is a major undertaking. Realizing that MRP/ERP vendors have spent years rejecting FCS, how could they overnight understand how to develop a new approach that includes FCS? Also, how much influence will the new FCS partner exert over the existing ERP influence? Years have been spent analyzing approaches to the integration of the two systems. Although a major concept has been developed, writing and implementing a system is yet another hurdle.

Merging ERP and FCS together is an interim process. While the trend of interfacing FCS/ERP by a series of multiple passes until both the material and capacity systems are feasible is a great improvement over the traditional approach using infinite capacity, a preferred approach for the clients is to have both the material and capacity functions in a single module so that capacity and material calculations are simultaneous in a single pass. To accomplish this will mean a complete revision in how MRP/ERP systems were originally designed. Until then, the best solution for clients is thoroughly to investigate interfaced solutions.

Many clients are committed to the long-term use of their existing MRP/ERP systems. In this case, a client interested in adding FCS capability requires investigating if the MRP/ERP vendor has developed capable FCS software. The alternative is the purchase of an independent FCS system that already interfaces or that the vendor commits to interfacing to the client's existing MRP/ERP. Clients should not conclude that the MRP/ERP supplier has interfaced a partner scheduling system that is best for the client application. Each company should evaluate the MRP-supplied FCS system to determine if it is a good fit for the company's application. The alternative is to consider purchasing an independent FCS/APS (Advanced Planning and Scheduling) system to interface with the existing MRP/ERP systems.

The predominant systems that are in vogue today, such as Supply Chain Management (SCM) and Enterprise Resource Planning (ERP), currently have the major influence over how manufacturing companies are managing their resources. Numerous system designations are available that add value and interface with the SCM and ERP systems. Examples in addition to FCS and APS are Manufacturing Execution Systems and Shop Floor Tracking. Many of them are difficult to distinguish by the designated name. Overlap in capability is prominent among these designations. As time progress, the ERP and SCM vendors will include some or all of these peripheral systems as integrated systems. As in the past, clients will have to decide when to purchase the entire package and when to elect to use an independent vendor. History seems to indicate that smaller companies that develop specialty packages usually have better functionality than those that adopt the packaged software by the large vendors. The decision becomes which is better—an all-encompassing integrated system or a best-of-breed collection of system modules.

Y2K

For several years companies have been actively instituting solutions to manage the millennium bug. Resources being exerted for this effort continue to increase. As noted daily on all news channels, the concern over the Y2K problem is enormous and the financial and personnel commitment to solving the problem is proportionally high. Interest in FCS systems during this corresponding period has also been very high. However, the implementation of FCS systems is not keeping pace with interest. The excessive financial and personnel commitment that companies have to make to solve the Y2K problem contributes to the slow implementation of FCS systems. The ERP and SCM stocks, which were elevated in the past several years, have recently experienced major declines, apparently because most companies have made commitments to solve the Y2K problem and orders are slowing.

The need to solve the Y2K problem has had a negative effect on FCS sales. We believe this period is ending and that by the year 2000 there will be a surge by manufacturing companies purchasing and implementing modern scheduling techniques. There will be a flurry of effort by the MRP/ERP suppliers to add scheduling capability. If they have not been working on a solution for several years, they will have to purchase it from an independent FCS supplier or be left behind. Scheduling will become the most important addition to the ERP chain of modules.

SUMMARY

Industry Week (*IW*) recently published the results of a census survey it conducted. It reported that Advanced Planning and

Scheduling (APS) was the area of technology most often cited by respondents as the next system to be implemented. The report stated that APS was cited by 47.6 percent of plant level respondents and was well ahead of the second most often cited on the list, which was to have Electronic Data Interchange (EDI) links to suppliers (39.7 percent). *Industry Week* went on to state that the rapid growth and use of the Internet would reduce the degree of EDI implementation in the future since the Internet is more accessible and less expensive.

In the past, FCS has experienced an extensive era of resistance. However, world-class competitiveness requires MRP/ERP users and vendors to reconsider their hard-line stance against FCS. They are realizing that there is a difference between planning and scheduling systems, and that both are needed. More and more vendors are in the process of integrating FCS into their existing packages. By early in the next decade, most if not all MRP/ERP vendors will be including Finite Capacity Scheduling. It will become a critical tool for competitive success.

Common sense is not common.
—WILL ROGERS

Selecting an Application: Finite Capacity Scheduling Methods

Bill Kirchmier, Data Based Systems
billk@databased.com

The question regarding finite capacity scheduling (FCS) is not so much "Is my company ready for FCS?" but "Can we afford to wait?" Companies that have implemented FCS systems and made the necessary cultural changes have reaped productivity improvements and realized competitive advantages.

I'd like to begin by quoting Laura D'Andrea Tyson, dean of the Haas School of Business at the University of California at Berkeley and previous economic advisor to President Clinton, who said: "Productivity growth is the key variable not

Reprinted from *APICS—The Performance Advantage*, August 1998, Volume 8, Number 8.

only in the trade-off between inflation and unemployment, but also in the economy's long-run growth performance. Over time, output growth is determined by the improvement in productivity."

Improved productivity through better utilization of resources is what finite capacity scheduling is all about.

FCS systems have evolved and matured over the past 10 years, and more than 100 packaged software alternatives are now commercially available. The capabilities and costs of these systems vary dramatically, with no single system reigning supreme. With the growth and success in the number of FCS systems, plus a continuing increase in installations by early adapters, many companies today use such scheduling methods.

But the emergence of FCS systems has created tension in the ranks of devoted MRP/MRP II/ERP users, with heated debates swirling about the value of FCS. In reality, however, there should be no conflict. MRP systems solve material and, to some degree planning problems, whereas FCS systems solve only scheduling problems. Minus the perceived conflict, MRP/ERP systems and FCS systems are truly natural partners.

To appreciate the value of FCS systems, one should realize that moving from traditional scheduling techniques to any FCS system will improve productivity, if appropriate cultural changes are implemented. Two of the major motivating factors for moving from traditional scheduling to FCS scheduling are the universal demand for short cycle times and predictability of delivery dates.

Many companies perceive the discipline required for implementing and maintaining FCS systems as being too great to justify moving to FCS. Ultimately, however, the commitment must be made. The increased success of companies that make the move will put pressure on competitive companies that stick with traditional scheduling.

EVALUATING FCS METHODS

The prominent scheduling methods used by the vast majority of FCS systems are as follows:

➤ Job-based.

➤ Resource-based.

➤ Event-based.

These terms are not universally established, and few standards exist in the industry; thus each of these terms can lead to assumptions that are not intended. To avoid misinterpretation, consider the methods within the concept presented and try not to read into it any ideas which the terms might suggest to you. The terms used to define the techniques are not important. What is important is to distinguish between the methods and how they function.

The scheduling methods are best distinguished by how each method selects the next task to be processed. The scheduling method selected by the vendor has a profound effect on the degree of modeling capability available for developing features and functions within the FCS system, which will serve as the user interfaces for modeling your application.

Of the three major methods, the job-based method is the most intuitive and is considered the easiest to implement. The primary objective of this method is to process the highest priority job first, then the second and so on. Any number of rules can be applied to determine job priority. But once the rule for establishing priority is selected, the job-based method will schedule all tasks of the first job out into the future prior to scheduling the next highest priority job.

You might think of this method as "block scheduling," because the user is blocking or freezing resources out into the future, reserving resources based on the established priority of each job.

The primary objective of the resource-based method is to schedule the bottleneck work centers to ensure that no wasted capacity exists in these areas. In other words, this method ensures that the critical resources have no gaps of unused capacity—a desirable feature since the bottleneck work center is a constraint. The noncritical resources are then scheduled. A subsequent objective of this method is to make sure the constrained resource always has work to be processed. Job priority is considered within this context.

The resource-based method is also commonly known as theory of constraints (TOC). I have not used the term TOC to describe this approach because the FCS vendors who promote TOC differ so greatly. TOC advocates seem to agree on the primary approach of how to perform the basic calculations for scheduling the bottleneck resources; however, no standards seem to exist among the various vendors for scheduling the noncritical resources. For this reason, the resource-based method is the most difficult of the methods to define in simple terms, or to evaluate with the other methods.

One major point of note differentiating the resource-based system from the job-based approach lies in the scheduling of the bottleneck resources, which is done at the task level in the resource-based method and not at the job level (as in the job-based method). The resource-based method blocks out time in the future; however, scheduling critical resources at the task level ensures that no gaps of wasted capacity will exist at critical resources.

The first scheduling pass of the bottleneck work centers may create unfeasibility for some of the noncritical resources. The conflicts are resolved by an iteration of forward and backward scheduling passes, but this results in an overall increase in cycle time and work in process. Thus the resource-based method functions best in applications where the bottleneck remains stationary at a single resource, as functionality tends to diminish with an increase in the number of bottlenecks and/or when bottlenecks tend to move between work centers.

Despite the obvious differences, there is a degree of convergence of the job-based and resource-based methods. Several job-based vendors have implemented routines to apply resource-scheduling techniques as an option within their system.

The event-based method uses true simulation as the basis of scheduling. A scheduling simulation system, by definition, progresses forward on a minute-by-minute basis (i.e., the event-based method is myopic; it does not look downstream). This means that the system only schedules what is visible at that moment in simulation time.

Competitive vendors will argue that the event-based approach does not allow for blocking out resources for high priority jobs. This is only a perception; actually, event-based systems perform better by applying advanced modeling techniques to improve capacity utilization and ensure resource availability for high priority jobs at the time they are needed.

A major objective of the event-based method is not to waste capacity if demand for the resource exists. This applies to both critical and noncritical resources. This statement should not be confused with the old accounting approach of: If the machine is empty, then fill it. The scheduling objective is to eliminate gaps of unused capacity only when demand exists for the resource.

The event-based method consistently demonstrates better throughput characteristics and resource utilization in comparisons I have witnessed between it and the other two prominent methods. It is also somewhat more difficult to implement; however, ongoing maintenance appears to be less than with the other two approaches.

CHOOSING WHICH IS RIGHT FOR YOU

Any of the three scheduling methods will greatly improve productivity and increase scheduling stability and predictability compared to the traditional infinite capacity approach. The scheduling method a company should choose is not easy to globally stipulate because of differences in companies' management styles and because experience in both scheduling techniques and computer technology is very company dependent.

Based on the comparisons I have witnessed, there is no consistency for comparing system cost with scheduling capability. It should also be noted that a cost disparity exists within each family of methods. Vendors naturally promote the features and benefits of the method they are selling. But in reality, few vendors understand the implications of the competitive methods, and this is a compelling reason why prospects should understand the playing field.

One of the most significant problems with implementing any FCS system is the resistance by personnel who have a vested interest in maintaining the status quo of the current method being used. The solution here is to start educating early to avoid downstream problems. Involve personnel in the decision process as early as possible. Education at all levels is an important factor in reducing the time and cost for installation of FCS systems.

The benefits of moving from traditional infinite scheduling to FCS are very apparent. Which FCS method or which vendor to choose is less obvious.

The noted business author Peter Drucker argues persuasively that "the measure of productivity is output per unit of time given finite resources."

The best criterion for evaluating FCS scheduling systems is the measure of capacity utilization. Systems that maximize capacity utilization for a given demand (i.e., minimize cycle time for fixed resources and fixed demand) will result in better overall performance, increased throughput, more scheduling stability, shorter cycle times, and reduced expediting.

The best way to compare scheduling methods is to create an actual subset of data of your company's application. This process has recently become known as a scripted demo. The same data can then be submitted to selected vendors in machine-readable format, which reduces the time needed to model the application. The results from the selected vendors can then be compared on equal terms.

No single vendor is best for all applications; therefore, you must be clear about the objective your company is striving to accomplish, and then develop a set of data that will ensure a good evaluation of these objectives. The alternative to an actual test of your application is to accept vendors' canned demonstrations using vendor data. Vendors generally do not like this scripted demo evaluation since it creates a measurable comparison and reduces their ability to concentrate on specific features they consider important to selling their system.

Chapter 2

Traditional
Scheduling Methods

*The world is moving so fast these days that the man who says
it can't be done is generally interrupted by someone doing it.*
—HARRY EMERSON FOSDICK

The youth of today, and of all previous generations, have
tried to change the world and make it a better place. Why is it
that the older we get, the only thing that we want to change
is the youth? The only thing certain in life is change. And
change can be triggered by new ideas and new technologies.
As we move through a discussion of the traditional scheduling methods, we will see how the methods of the past have
grown and developed through changes coming from many
directions.

The history of scheduling over the past 100 years has
forced us through numerous technological transitions. A century ago, production processes were labor intensive, and
maximizing throughput was simply a matter of cracking the

whip more often. The more productivity we got out of the work force, the better the financial results. However, since then, technology has changed the workplace dramatically. Technology has offered us new methodologies for planning and scheduling. Additionally, technology has shifted the focus away from labor toward machinery and materials as being the critical resource. Today, labor is seldom more than 10 percent of the value-added content of the products we produce. Materials and machinery have taken the dominant role. And their efficient use requires scheduling tools, not just the crack of a whip.

Scheduling technology of 100 years ago was composed of a list of jobs on a piece of paper. Today we simultaneously process hundreds and even thousands of jobs through a facility. And the tools have correspondingly changed. The list of jobs was replaced by Economic Order Quantity (EOQ), which used a reorder point system for planning and scheduling. Then, with the post–World War II years came the advent of the computer, which allowed us to install linear programming (LP), and later Material Requirements Planning (MRP) dispatch lists for the planning and scheduling process. It is now time for the next wave, the separation of the planning and scheduling technology. Material Requirements Planning (MRP) and some of its competitors like Theory of Constraints (TOC) still make excellent planners, but the scheduling process for the next era will be managed by FCS.

This chapter describes the various scheduling methods being used in the prominently marketed FCS systems. A description of the traditional infinite capacity method will be used to assist in making the distinction between the old and the new. The process for selecting the best FCS system for you will be described in Chapter 4.

TRADITIONAL SCHEDULING METHODS

Infinite capacity backward pass has been the traditional scheduling method accepted by Material Requirements Planning (MRP) and its more encompassing big brother Manufacturing Resources Planning (MRP II) scheduling systems. Although out-of-date, the history and use of infinite scheduling cannot be ignored. In the early 1960s, MRP began as a material planning system. The innovators of MRP systems foresaw the benefits of computer-based management of material requirements and took steps to make it a reality. At that time, the total cost of a computer system was in the millions and the system was pitifully slow in relation to present capability. As everyone knows, the cost of the central processing unit (CPU), main memory, and disk space has continued to drop and the power and speed have continued to increase.

Ray Kurzweil, in *The Age of Spiritual Machines*, points out the remarkable phenomenon that has been driving the acceleration of computing for the past 40 years:

Gordon Moore, an inventor of the integrated circuit and then chairman of Intel, noted in 1965 that the surface area of a transistor (as etched on an integrated circuit) was being reduced by approximately 50 percent every twelve months. In 1975, he was widely reported to have revised this observation to eighteen months. Moore claims that his 1975 update was to twenty-four months, and that does appear to be a better fit to the data.

The result is that every two years, you can pack twice as many transistors on an integrated circuit. This doubles both the number of components on a chip as well as its speed. Since the cost of an integrated circuit is fairly constant, the implication is that every two years you can get twice as much circuitry running at twice the speed for the same price. For many applications, that's an effective quadrupling of the value. The observation holds true for every type of circuit, from memory chips to computer processors.

This insightful observation has become known as Moore's Law on Integrated Circuits, and the remarkable phenomenon of the law has been driving the acceleration of computing for the past forty years.[1]

Material Requirements Planning (MRP) succeeded in replacing the manual systems and the EOQ-based systems. Manufacturing Resources Planning (MRP II) made additional advances and integrated the financial and engineering elements into the planning and scheduling process. However, since the foundation was already set with MRP, MRP II had less difficulty being accepted. Somewhere along the way, developers noted that in order to plan material it would also be necessary to consider capacity. At that time computer power was still very limited and expensive. Even if serious thought had been given to using modern scheduling methods, the computer power available at that time would not have been sufficient to perform the calculations or to be cost-effective.

The infinite capacity backward pass (ICBP) approach that was chosen as the method to be implemented was appropriate based on the technology resources available. In this

---

[1] From *The Age of Spiritual Machines* (New York: Viking, 1999), a fascinating book on the evolution of computing, including Ray Kurzweil's predictions on the future of computing and when computers will match the power of the human brain.

book ICBP is considered to be a planning method, not a scheduling method, although most vendors and users refer to it as a scheduling method. The inability of ICBP to schedule is only one of the reasons FCS is now threatening to dislodge this incumbent.

RESISTANCE TO CHANGE

The typical employee involved in the management of material and capacity has invested numerous years in the concepts developed and promoted by MRP vendors. This large investment in time and commitment to both software and training makes it difficult for the individual to move to a new and controversial technology. This is due mainly to the investment required both by the employee and by the vendors who would like to keep making profits on their existing investment.

The resistance by many users to move forward and accept a computer-based scheduling approach has been excessive. The detractors were eager to rush in and point to any malfunction or problem exhibited by any of the new scheduling systems. This pattern of resistance is typical of new systems and the same pattern for the past 10 years has been and still is slowing the progress of FCS. A large portion of the user population commonly referred to as "late adapters" typically resists new innovative products.

Even when one is convinced that it is time to move to a new technology, the question of how to accomplish the task seems overwhelming. To justify moving from existing software to a new software system, particularly where many personnel must invest time to implement the new software, is difficult for companies. For instance, word processing systems have been in use for years. The benefits have been great and very few people would even consider using a typewriter anymore. But the trauma associated with moving a company from a current word processing system to a new word processing product is considerable. There are numerous barriers that need to be crossed to justify the change, such as:

➤ Purchase cost.

➤ Implementation cost.

➤ Disruption.

➤ Additional costs that cannot be identified.

**Systems are like politicians;
the incumbent has the advantage
of remaining in place.**

Human inertia that tends to maintain the status quo is normally a stabilizing factor. However, when a positive new paradigm appears, this same inertia slows progress. There are many examples of this syndrome, as in the move from horses to automobiles. Bill Kirchmier's grandfather was a good example. He owned a livery stable in a small town in Indiana and went bankrupt thinking the automobile would not succeed.

Having made the decision to use ICBP in the past, it is time to identify why it is now necessary to move to a better scheduling procedure. What are the problems and shortcomings of ICBP?

THE SHORTCOMINGS OF ICBP

There are two fundamental problems with ICBP. The first problem is that ICBP yields unfeasible results. The assumption of infinite capacity is erroneous, at least in most work centers. If infinite capacity did exist in all work centers, then there would never be a scheduling problem. Infinite capacity implies that any demand appearing at any work center at any time can be accomplished upon arrival at the work center. We all know this is not reality.

The second problem is that MRP uses a fixed *queue allowance* for each operation. A queue is a waiting list and the queue allowance is the estimated waiting time before starting each task. These MRP queue estimates are an attempt to approach actual shop conditions; the result is an unrealistic and unwanted increase in cycle time. The queue allowance spreads the workload in an attempt to make up for the fact that MRP does not recognize that each task is going to have a unique waiting time; MRP attempts to average out the waiting time by creating an average queue allowance.

The following description is taken from the JobTime Plus users' manual issued by JobTime Systems Inc.:

> The MRP master scheduling backward pass method and fixed queue allowance techniques are inaccurate. Many tasks do not have to queue. In addition, actual task queue times can vary greatly. Such variation can be 0% to 1000% of the average queue time. Even in a stable environment, the queue time for each task varies. When a new task arrives at a work center and joins a queue, you can estimate actual queue time. It will be the sum of the processing times of all the tasks already waiting in the queue line when the new task arrives. However, higher

priority tasks may arrive and jump ahead in the queue. Only a comprehensive simulation of queuing behavior can accurately estimate queue time for each task.

Queue times also depend on additional conditions such as required multiple resources, matching setups, split lots, assembly jobs, release dates, variations in processing rate and variations in material quality. In addition, capacity changes regularly by shift and by day of the week. Capacity is also adjusted temporarily through overtime assignments.

Virtually every MRP system backward schedules each work order from its due date and implicitly assumes that capacity is unlimited. MRP's forward scheduling starts from release date and also assumes capacity is unlimited. Notice that these are the same assumptions made by most PERT/CPM systems. MRP does not provide an accurate way of estimating the waiting time between tasks and therefore cannot accurately estimate finish dates.

MRP schedules each job as if it were the only job in the shop. It loads each task on each work center without regard for capacity limits. The technical developer of a prominent MRP system once told us, "It's easy. We print a capacity requirement report that shows under-load and overload conditions. The shop manager just has a meeting every morning with sales to resolve the overload or under-load for the day." Do you see anything wrong in this picture? Traditional PERT/CPM and MRP systems have one flaw in common. Both systems are based on models that assume infinite capacity.

THE INFINITE CAPACITY DILEMMA

First analyze Table 2.1 using the discussion in the following paragraph. This defines the parameters that will be used to

Table 2.1 Infinite Capacity Dilemma

Job Number	Arrival Time	Task Duration
Job 1	8:00 A.M.	1.0 Hours
Job 2	8:00 A.M.	1.5 Hours
Job 3	12:30 P.M.	2.5 Hours
Job 4	12:30 P.M.	1.5 Hours
Job 5	2:30 P.M.	1.5 Hours

demonstrate the primary problem with infinite capacity scheduling. Prior to viewing Figure 2.1, you should personally solve the problem based on the conditions. Do not violate any of the constraints. Then view the figures to compare your solution to the ICBP solution.

The example includes five tasks from five separate jobs. The due date for each job is today at 4:00 P.M., which is the end of the workday. The tasks are to be processed through a single work center. The total processing time for all five tasks is eight hours. Note the arrival times of the tasks and the duration times for each task in Table 2.1. No work is available at the work center between 10:30 A.M. and 12:30 P.M. and the work center must remain idle during that time period. Since only one resource is available and two hours of capacity are not used, two hours of work are forced into the following day. Now consider Figure 2.1 and see how the infinite capacity method would solve the problem.

The ICBP method ignores the condition that only a single resource exists in the work center. All tasks are complete when due, which is today at exactly 4:00 P.M. Designers of systems that use the ICBP method realize that this is not feasible and make adjustments in an attempt to cure the problem caused by this incorrect assumption.

The proposed solution to correct the erroneous assump-

Task

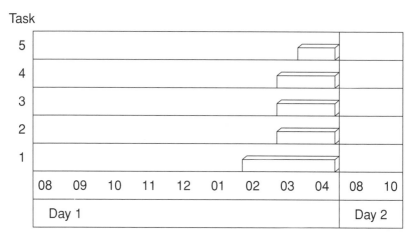

Figure 2.1   Infinite Capacity Scheduling—The Solution Is Unfeasible.

tion is yet another incorrect assumption. The second assumption is that queue times are the same for all tasks. Standard tasks are stipulated for each center, and each task passing through the work center is assigned this standard. The standard queue is based on data from past experience. The result is to extend job cycle times and to increase work in progress (WIP) more than is needed or wanted.

The other fundamental problem is the backward pass approach. The backward pass approach begins scheduling on the due date of the job and works backward on a task-by-task basis. It is assumed that each previous task must be complete prior to starting the following task. This is a sequential process. The calculation to determine when the first task must begin in order to complete the final task and meet the due date is very simple. If, however, the processing time available between today's date and the due date is greater

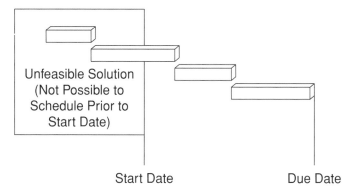

Figure 2.2 Backward Pass Dilemma Associated with Infinite Capacity.

than the actual time available, an unfeasible condition will exist as noted in Figure 2.2.

The alternative FCS solution is very simple: Two tasks arrive at the work center at 8:00 A.M. and work can begin on either task. Work on the second task can begin upon completion of the first task. No work is available upon completion of the second task; since no demand exists, the work center remains idle until 12:30 P.M., when additional work arrives. At the end of the workday, the remaining work must wait until the next day to be processed. Figure 2.3 is one of a number of feasible solutions.

As a proponent of infinite capacity scheduling, you have the challenge of advising your president that the company's scheduling results are based on the assumption of having infinite capacity and therefore all of the calculations produced from the company's MRP system are unfeasible. If your company is making a profit using unfeasible scheduling, think of the improvement if calculations were based on actual capacity and the schedules were feasible.

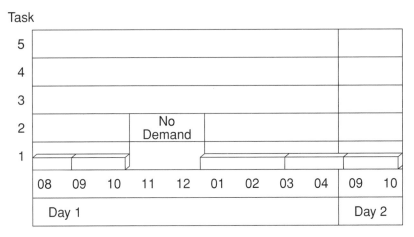

Figure 2.3 Feasible FCS Schedule of Table 2.1 Conditions.

FCS Scheduling Methodologies

Next we look at the primary scheduling methods available from FCS suppliers. The analysis methods used will encompass most of the commercially available systems. The field is relatively new but the number of vendors has been growing rapidly. The three main methods of FCS scheduling have been used for 10 or more years. They are logical approaches based on the human thought processes and all yield feasible results. Other methods may also appear; however, we cannot clearly identify any other basic method at this time. The three methods are well established and make up a large majority of the methodologies being applied by FCS vendors. Any of the three methods is capable of producing feasible results.

The three prominent FCS methods are:

➤ Job-based.

➤ Event-based.

➤ Resource-based.

These designations were derived as a result of an RFP (request for proposal) from McDermott International in the early 1990s. At this time FCS scheduling was in its infancy. Very few vendors existed. The contact at McDermott was Ken Cybulsky, who has a master's degree in operations research and understands and is well versed in scheduling techniques.

McDermott International manufactures offshore oil well drilling rigs and other heavy equipment. Designing and building offshore platforms is equivalent to building ships, and each drilling platform requires a high degree of customizing. The sequencing of the production operations through the selected manufacturing facility was difficult to schedule. McDermott was interested in improving the throughput. This sparked the research department to create a discrete event simulation (DES) scheduling tool of its shop in Ireland. A simulation language was used as the tool to develop an in-house scheduling solution.

The scheduling tool was judged to be successful and useful; however, it required a person at the site who was experienced with the simulation language. Training or supplying a trained person with simulation experience capable of managing the scheduling system could not be justified.

McDermott's experience with the in-house scheduling system was promising, and a set of specifications was developed and sent to more than 10 FCS vendors. The RFP included very detailed drawings of the plant; the sequences of operations and all other criteria were well defined.

The project was interesting and since Ken and his fellow employees had already solved the problem, they had a benchmark for judging vendor results. Each vendor was asked to model the shop and prepare to demonstrate the results at McDermott's research center in Ohio.

The vendor demonstrations were planned in conjunction with an annual meeting of McDermott personnel from around the world. Three of the vendors responding to the RFP were invited to demonstrate their software. There were two objectives: (1) to expose personnel at the meeting to modern scheduling techniques and (2) to locate an acceptable solution that would be cost-effective.

Ken's research and the demonstrations led to his defining the three categories of FCS methodologies. As time passed these categories became known as job-based, event-based, and resource-based.

Bill Kirchmier has adapted the scheduling notations Ken selected and has since used them in seminars to distinguish between the different methods. The results of the performance of the different vendor packages will not be discussed since they were all in their infancy and earlier success or failure should not influence today's decisions. Bill is grateful to have had the opportunity to work with and learn from Ken Cybulsky and McDermott International. The experience influenced his creating a seminar to explain the functionality of the various methods. The seminar has been continuously updated to stay current with new vendor features and functions.

FCS METHODS

Prior to describing the characteristics of each of the three FCS scheduling methods, this chapter describes the corresponding point of departure of the methods. Each method is built around an information base of three data files:

➢ Resource file.

➢ Routing file.

➢ Job file.

The resource file, or work center file, contains information about the capacity available to perform work. The file distinguishes by shift the number of workstations (resources) available and the number of shifts being worked by each work center.

The routing file defines the sequence of events a job must pass through to be complete. A job contains tasks (operations) that must be processed in a logical sequence for a job to be complete. Routing files also include constraint information; however, constraint information may also reside in other files.

The job file contains at minimum the following data fields: release date, due date, quantity, user priority, and customer ID if the product is for a customer (if not for a customer, the part can be identified as stock).

The three files are client application dependent. The conditions and constraints are defined for the client's unique application.

Each method has a primary and unique approach in how the next job or task is selected. Also, each method has a unique effect on how features and functions are implemented in the systems. The variances in functionality of each method will be discussed later, after the basic methods have been explained.

JOB-BASED METHOD (JBM)

The job-based method uses job priority as the criterion for deciding which is the next job to be processed. The job-based method selects the highest-priority job first and schedules all tasks for that job prior to scheduling the next job. This method is similar to block scheduling because you are blocking out or freezing resources out into the future. After scheduling the top job, the next highest priority job is scheduled and so on until all jobs have been scheduled.

The job-based method schedules at the job level. This differentiates it from the event-based method that schedules at the task level.

Setting job priorities has traditionally been a manual process in MRP systems. Manual priorities are available in FCS systems, but FCS systems have an additional ability to dynamically set priorities by examining the conditions of the job mix while the schedule is being created. The job-based system generates schedules based on priorities regardless of whether the priorities were determined dynamically by the system or set by the user. It should be noted that user-set priorities override system-set priorities, and this diminishes the ability of the system to deliver the functionality for which it was designed. A good procedure is to avoid manually setting any priorities on the first scheduling run, review the results of the schedule, and then selectively modify priorities and recalculate the schedule.

Work center load conditions in Figure 2.4 will be used to demonstrate how the job-based method would schedule two jobs through two work centers, A and B.

The constraints are:

WC	A	B
Number of Resources	2	1

Job	1	2
Priority	Highest	Next Highest

Figure 2.4   Work Center Load Conditions.

1. Work center A has two resources, or workstations (WS).

2. Work center B has one resource.

3. Job 1 has a user-set higher priority than job 2.

4. Each job must be sequenced through work center A prior to processing in work center B.

This same set of conditions will later be used to show how the event-based system would process the identical work. This comparison will demonstrate the basic difference in how the two methods determine sequencing of work through the shop. These very basic decisions have a significant impact on how secondary decisions are made that determine features and functions of an FCS system.

When the scheduling cycle begins, the job-based system would select job 1 first since job 1 priority is higher than job 2 priority. As described in Figure 2.5, task 1 of job 1 is processed in WC A; upon completion of task 1, work would proceed to work center B for processing task 2. Task 2 would have no delay since there is no competition at this point in time in work center B. This completes the processing

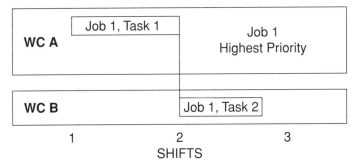

Figure 2.5 Job-Based Scheduling—Loading Job 1, the Highest-Priority Job.

required for job 1, and the system looks for the next highest priority job to schedule.

The system now schedules job 2, the next highest priority job (Figure 2.6). Task 1 of job 2 requires a resource in work center A. A workstation is available, so the first task of job 2 is loaded. Task 1 of job 2 finishes prior to task 1 of job 1. Task 2 of job 2 is now ready to be processed in work center B. Work center B has time open and could start the operation; however, it could not finish the operation without impacting the higher-priority job 1. Loading and stopping job 2 is not considered as an option in this example. The processing of task 2 of job 2 must be moved to the finish time of task 2 of job 1. This leaves some unused capacity in work center B.

Demand that would fit into and occupy some or all of the time available in work center B may materialize as more jobs are scheduled. Wasted capacity needs to be minimized. Job-based systems use backward and forward passes to refine the schedule and minimize wasted capacity. The degree of success in reducing wasted capacity is a function of many variables, including how the vendor system manages secondary feature and function decisions.

48

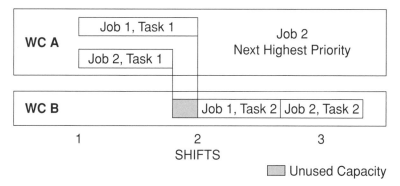

Figure 2.6 Job-Based Scheduling—Loading Job 2, Task 2.

EVENT-BASED METHOD (EBM)

Visualize the EBM method by viewing the work centers as portrayed in Figure 2.7. Think of the work centers as being in a vertical pattern with each work center moving forward in time. The tasks in Figure 2.7 represent demand for resources that arrive at work centers A, B, and C at time t_0 through t_5.

At the beginning of the schedule at time t_0, demand exists for work centers A and C. Since there is no contention for either resource, both tasks begin processing at time t_0. Time progresses to t_1, at which time another task appears in work center C. WC C has two idle workstations, there is no contention in the work center and the new task begins processing.

At time t_2, a task appears in WC A, and since there is no contention for the second workstation the task can begin processing. At time t_3, a task appears at WC B. WC B has a single workstation that is currently idle so the task begins processing. Time progresses to t_4, when a second task appears in work center B; since the only workstation in WC B is occupied, the task must wait in the queue until the other task

49

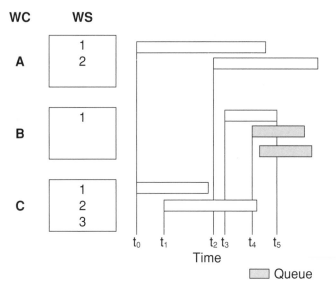

Figure 2.7 Interpretation of Time-Based Loading of Event-Based Method.

completes processing. Prior to the first two tasks finishing, a third task arrives at WC B. At this point two tasks are in the queue at WC B.

When the WC B resource completes processing its first task at time t_5, the system must make a decision about which of the two tasks in the queue will be processed next. The next task to be processed is a function of many other constraints established in the model. A default condition will be defined by the EBM system that will determine which task will be processed based on secondary feature and function decisions. As an example, if both tasks have the same priority, the second task would process next. If the third task has a higher priority, then it would precede task two. The modeling options are endless, leaving the strategy under the client's control.

In this example we see that the criteria for selection are at the task (operation) level as opposed to the job level. This is an important distinction. No downstream work assignments are made. Scheduling at the task level is more granular and increases the selection options available.

The conditions defined in Table 2.1 and Figure 2.4 will now be applied to the event-based method. Figures 2.8 through 2.10 will be used to describe the sequencing of the example. At the beginning of the scheduling sequence, the EBM views all the demand for all of the work centers. Based on demand it then makes decisions regarding which task to process at each work center. In our example (Figure 2.8), two tasks are in the queue for WC A. Since there are two workstations available, both tasks are loaded for processing. No demand exists for WC B, so the work center remains idle.

Time progresses with no activity until task 1 of job 2 completes processing. Job 2 is now available for processing at WC B (Figure 2.9). Since no contention exits at WC B at this time, the task is loaded for processing. Time progresses to the completion of task 1 of job 1. This is a high-priority job; however, no capacity is available in WC B to begin processing the

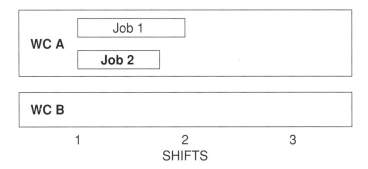

Figure 2.8 Event-Based Loading Sequence.

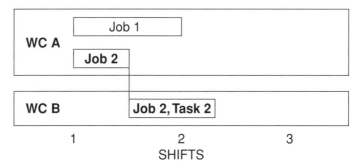

Figure 2.9 Event-Based Scheduling—Loading Job 2, Task 2 in Work Center B.

task. The resource is occupied by task 2 of job 2. When task 2 of job 2 is completed (Figure 2.10), task 2 of job 1 is loaded for processing.

The major distinction between the JBM and the EBM is that the JBM concentrates on getting priority jobs completed on time at the expense of wasted capacity, whereas the EBM concentrates on high utilization when demand exists. This does not imply that priority jobs are not considered by the EBM. Proponents for each method will argue that their method is better. However, we doubt that this argument will ever be settled; there are simply too many variables, and both methods yield feasible solutions. The method best for your application is a function of the company's management style, strategy, and numerous features and functions that will be discussed in Chapter 4.

Discrete event simulation (DES) planning systems are the predecessor to DES scheduling systems. Numerous companies have for years marketed discrete event simulation planning systems. Discrete event simulation production planning models were usually based on statistical data. The more advanced DES systems also offered graphic animation

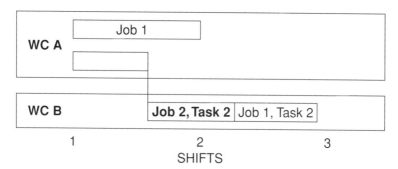

Figure 2.10 Event-Based Scheduling—Loading Job 1, Task 2 in Work Center B.

tools to exhibit the results so that management could visibly observe the flow of jobs through the manufacturing process as determined by the discrete event simulation.

This approach proved to be successful and popular for factory planning. A day, a week, or a month of production time could be reduced to minutes with animation tools at a very small expense. This type of simulation allows the factory flow to be tested in many different configurations and product mixes by utilizing variable capacity and demand conditions to perform what-if scenarios. Management can visually view the results in animation mode.

The use of statistical data may be adequate for planning a manufacturing process, but deterministic data is needed for short interval scheduling to be effective.

Most DES companies were slow to see the opportunity for deterministic event-based simulation as a tool for manufacturing scheduling. Now the EBM discrete event simulation systems are a major factor in the scheduling industry.

The DES planning tools were almost exclusively based on a simulation language. Examples of simulation languages include GPSS, SLAM, SYMON, and SIMSCRIPT, and there are numerous others. However, a simulation language is not a prerequisite to building a DES scheduling tool. For example, Bill Kirchmier's partner at JobTime Systems Inc., Paul Wyman, created JobTime Plus in the early 1980s without using a simulation language.

Simulation languages allow for a model that views the activity as if it were happening in real time. Each language was created with the intent of evaluating activity over time in small increments. The smaller the increment of time, the more accurate the results. There is a practical limit: One minute is the accepted unit of time for most scheduling applications. Since most tasks occupy less than an hour of processing, using increments of hours or days yields unrealistic results due to excessive rounding. Although operations exist that exceed a day or even several days, they are the exception in manufacturing scheduling and the computer power available today has little or no negative effect for calculating long operations down to the minute.

Simulation tools operate in a myopic mode. This means that the system schedules only what is visible at that moment in simulation time. It does not look downstream and make decisions at some future time. Features can be built into simulation models that will allow for the control of downstream conditions, but not by blocking out time in the future. Scheduling methods that block out and load resources for some future time are not simulation systems in the technical sense.

The use of computers for modeling many kinds of activity is now usually referred to as simulation. This is a loose definition of simulation and has diluted what the term *simulation* had meant in engineering circles for many years.

Today, the reference to simulation is most often a computer model that represents a real-life event but is not time dependent. Most computer applications referred to as simulations are simply modeling a set of conditions in a non-dynamic mode. The structural design of buildings is a good example. Engineers design structures using structural calculations that meet static conditions; however, a simulation is required to test the design under dynamic load conditions that are caused by earthquakes. The dynamic forces for the simulation are accomplished by using recorded seismic data from previous earthquakes; these recordings are imposed on the static design. The static structure can be tested based on the force of one or more earthquakes to determine what would have happened to the structure had it been subjected to the actual earthquake. Dynamic factors are involved in these simulations—frequencies, amplitude and direction of forces, or other time-based variables. In California and some other states, a dynamic structural computer analysis is required to obtain a building permit for most commercial structures.

Other physical examples of dynamic, time-dependent simulations are the testing of vessels moving through fluids, or an airfoil in a wind tunnel. Some of the America's Cup boats were designed using computer simulation.

In 1962, Bill Kirchmier was personally involved with the sale and installation of five 900-horsepower vertical turbine pumps that were to be installed on the Columbia River upstream from the Arrow Lakes Dam in British Columbia. We questioned the consultant's original design of the pump house as being at risk of destroying the pumps from vortex vibration. With engineering help from Bill's employer, Fairbanks Morse & Co., the engineers were convinced to conduct a simulation test. The test was conducted using very small pumps—the pumps and the pump house were dimensionally scaled to represent the proposed pump house design. The final design of the pump house was altered as a result of the simulation, resulting in hundreds of thousands of dollars being saved. Simulation offers the opportunity to evaluate solutions that otherwise would not be considered.

The EBM qualifies as a dynamic time-based simulation since it makes scheduling decisions as in real time; this distinguishes simulation systems from scheduling systems that predetermine conditions at some future time and block out resources based on the predetermined condition. This distinction does not diminish the value of non–event-based systems, but it notes the inherent differences in how schedules are calculated. Since the term simulation is used to describe almost any computer model, it is necessary that a distinction be made between time-based simulation and static modeling.

An inherent characteristic of the EBM is the avoidance of wasted capacity if demand for a resource exists. Please note that this statement is not recommending the old accounting approach, "If the machine is empty, then fill it." The technique is to ensure that no gaps of unused capacity are allowed if there is demand for the resource.

Any of the three FCS methods will greatly improve productivity and increase scheduling stability and predictability beyond that offered by the traditional infinite capacity approach. It is not possible to globally stipulate the scheduling method a company should choose because of the many variables involved. Chapter 4 is devoted to selecting a system.

RESOURCE-BASED METHOD (RBM)

The resource-based method (RBM) uses the Theory of Constraints (TOC) approach of scheduling the bottleneck work center (WC) first. Scheduling the bottleneck WC is done at the task level. As in the EBM, the bottleneck will remain busy and ensure that no wasted capacity will exist in the critical resource. The RBM assumes that all noncritical work centers have infinite capacity. If there is only a single bottleneck and the noncritical work centers actually do have infinite capacity, then the assumption is valid. However, if some of the noncritical work centers have short-term (wandering) bottlenecks, they are likely to cause the schedule to be unfeasible when using the assumption of infinite capacity.

We have not used the term *TOC* to describe this method because vendors who promote the TOC approach differ so greatly. They seem to agree on the primary approach in how they make the basic selection of the bottleneck, but after scheduling the critical resources, no standard seems to exist as to the scheduling approach for the noncritical resources. For this reason we define the method as resource-based. This method is the most difficult of the various methods to define in simple terms due to the different positions of vendors that adhere to the basic TOC approach.

The TOC approach has been around longer than most FCS systems and has greatly benefited the companies that have manually implemented the method. The basic concept of TOC introduced by Dr. Eli Goldratt in *The Goal* points out that bottleneck resources need to be assured of constantly having a queue to avoid wasting resources. Maximum performance is realized when the bottleneck work centers are fully utilized.

The assumption that noncritical resources are not bottlenecks is an acceptable assumption when the scheduling process is manual, even though assuming infinite capacity in noncritical work centers is not accurate for all conditions.

Manual scheduling does not have the ability to support the calculation power required to finite schedule all work centers. Therefore the assumption of infinite capacity in work centers that are usually not bottlenecks is an acceptable approach. To reach the degree of accuracy required to finitely calculate all resources requires computer power. Using computers to implement the RBM allows for the finite calculation of noncritical work centers. The term *resource-based* has been introduced to make the distinction of including noncritical work centers as finite resources so that feasible schedules are ensured.

We no longer classify TOC as an FCS scheduling method. Rather, we now consider TOC as a technique that can be applied not only by RBM but also by both JBM and EBM. The basic TOC approach of scheduling the bottleneck work centers prior to scheduling noncritical work centers remains intact. The ability to move beyond the assumption of infinite capacity at noncritical resources is the reason that resource-based scheduling is used rather than TOC in our designation of methods.

Companies comparing computerized resource-based methods should clearly distinguish between ones that assume infinite capacity for noncritical WCs and systems that accurately define capacity constraints at all work centers. We do not consider computer-based systems that do not define capacity in all work centers to be FCS.

In summary, RBM schedules bottleneck work centers first, and then schedules noncritical resources. Conflicts are resolved by performing forward and backward passes. Infinite capacity assumptions are not made; work center capacities are finitely calculated through the entire time horizon for all resources. Resulting schedules are feasible.

FCS Systems of the Future

Finite Capacity Scheduling is a very active software sector. Vendors are actively adding capabilities. Additional scheduling approaches may become available that do not exactly fit into any of the three methods discussed. Some of the new capabilities are sophisticated scheduling techniques that are designed to solve specific difficult scheduling problems. The computer power available today is allowing advanced techniques to be applied to solving specific and difficult problems.

One example of particular interest is the genetic algorithm approach. We searched for a good brief definition and we found one in the Glossary of Ray Kurzweil's *The Age of Spiritual Machines*.

> Genetic algorithm—A model of machine learning that derives its behavior from a metaphor of the mechanisms of evolution in nature. Within a program, a population of simulated "individuals" are created and undergo a process of evolution in a simulated competitive environment.

Change the word *individuals* to *entity* in the definition and the concept becomes more realistic in defining the manufacturing world. The concept of genetic evolution can be (and is being) used as a tool to successfully evaluate nonbiological domains.

A scheduling-related interpretation of this definition might be a scheduling problem that would require multiple iterations, allowing for the evolution of the many possibilities. This approach arrives at the theoretical best sequence of operations. The key word is *evolution*. The scheduling programs are designed to select the best results and proceed to the next generation.

Genetic algorithm scheduling, as the name implies, is based on biological genetic propagation. Genetic scheduling is essentially a parallel analogy to biological genetics. Both are evolutionary processes. The conditions that affect offspring are random in both cases.

The objective in genetic scheduling is to test all possible combinations of feasible conditions and then select the optimum solution from the many feasible solutions. The number of options at any moment is so large it is essentially infinite. Biological propagation at times will produce cancers or other undesirable effects. Genetic scheduling can also produce undesirable results. Constraints can be inserted to prohibit solutions that would obviously drive the schedule down a route of diminishing returns. However, inserting constraints may also eliminate some desirable solutions.

Genetic algorithm scheduling is by nature a system that seeks optimal solutions; the term *optimal solutions* in the world of scheduling is vague and overused though and deserves a dedicated section.

This book is written to assist companies in understanding and selecting modern scheduling technology and genetic algorithms needed to be included in the discussion. However, due to the complexity and high cost of developing and implementing genetic scheduling, the amount of text devoted to it is limited since the book is more focused on the majority of clients, not the high-end clients. As time progresses, genetic scheduling systems will become less costly and more adaptable to a broader range of prospects. Since genetic algorithms are computer intensive, the continued trend of faster and cheaper computer power will also support the propagation of genetic scheduling.

> Technology transfer delivers a
> manufacturing scheduling technique based
> on genetic algorithm theory. The process
> fragments and recombines solutions, while
> discarding the least efficient ones, until it
> has a winning hand.
>
> —MARTHA K. RAYMOND, "Gin Rummy
> Tactics Win on the Factory Floor,"
> *American Machinist*, December 1995

Deere & Company utilizes the form of FCS called genetic algorithm theory to compute flexible systems and then optimizes on those schedules to come up with the most optimal schedule for its facility.

> The software generates very efficient
> schedules, and we're convinced that the
> investment was paid off within the first
> year.
>
> —BILL FULKERSON, staff analyst,
> Deere & Company[2]

Yet another example of a discipline on the horizon that is being used to evaluate complexity is chaos theory. This is a discipline that deals with unpredictable behavior and patterns of emergent behavior in complex systems. Scheduling problems that consist of many resources, jobs, operations, and constraints fit the definition of a complex system. This

---

[2] Taken from an article entitled "John Deere Runs on Chaos" in the November 1998 issue of *Fast Company*.

type of problem requires evaluation by nonlinear processes, not utilizing our normal linear thinking. To successfully evaluate and manage complex production facilities in a business requires the simultaneous evaluation of many conditions. These include the constant demand to reduce cycle times and other conditions that generate profits. The emerging technology of genetic algorithms and chaos theory combined with increasing computer power is the wave of the future for scheduling solutions and other complex problems.

An example of chaos can be visualized by observing water flowing from a faucet in laminar flow. You have seen the effect many times: As the water descends from the faucet the diameter of the stream gets smaller. Consider the question, how far does the stream have to flow before it disappears? Obviously the stream does not disappear; what happens is that the flow changes from laminar flow to turbulent flow. Turbulent flow is an area that has baffled mathematicians for years. We now know from chaos theory that conditions in turbulent flow are random and unpredictable; however, the turbulence does remain within a limited and definable boundary. This liquid flow pattern has a parallel in other complex environments including complex scheduling problems.

The objective in scheduling is to maximize throughput for existing demand without violating any constrains. Like the column of falling water that enters a state of chaos and becomes turbulent, there is an equivalent chaotic limit in a manufacturing facility that is pushed to its extreme. The point of maximum throughput for the stream of water is the point just prior to the turbulence. The point of maximum production throughput for the manufacturing facility is analogous to the flow example. Pushed beyond this point, production predictability becomes chaotic and indeterminate.

This concept can be used to avoid production inefficiency by not exceeding physically limiting conditions.

These concepts may seem esoteric if you have not investigated the new technologies. However, the use of these technologies in the future will play a large role in improving manufacturing production made possible by the continuing increase in computer power at lower cost.

Summary

> Because the Optiflex system knows the configuration of every planter that will be built over the next 15 days, module leaders can schedule work with near-perfect efficiency.
>
> —Paul Roberts describing John Deere's
> FCS environment[3]

The John Deere Seeding Group of Deere & Company, the world's largest maker of farm machinery, produces planters in 45 different models and 1.7 million options. Deere uses FCS to schedule production so carefully that every permutation can be built on the same assembly line. The company found that FCS facilitated inventory reductions; allowed machines to be moved closer together, thus reducing handling time; and initiated employee functional integration. The FCS system anticipates and schedules resource demands, allowing the scheduling of work to near-perfect efficiencies. John Deere

---

[3] Ibid. Optiflex is a product of Optimax Systems Corporation, which is now merged into I2 Technologies, Inc.

realized that day-to-day scheduling decisions could not come from the top. Now the company distributes authority and information throughout the company to where the incentives reside. And quality turns out to be the area that is the most positively affected by the FCS environment.

> We know a week ahead of time when a new kind of planter frame is coming. We know what needs to be done, and it gives us a chance to adjust.
> —BRAD DYKEMAN, Deere & Company[4]

Finite Capacity Scheduling is continuously being updated and modified. As time progresses, the three methods are converging in capability although they are very different. Each has unique characteristics and users need to learn how to evaluate the various systems for their specific application. Each camp will cite conditions that demonstrate that their method is superior. These arguments may appear logical when isolated from the total scheduling problem. The objective is to select the system that best fits your company's overall requirements. Do not get trapped in concentrating on a single feature or function. The ultimate goal is to maximize the use of your company's resources to meet the company strategy. A comprehensive evaluation of the various systems for scheduling your company's data is the best way to determine which vendor is best for your application.

The development of scheduling systems is currently very active. Many groups are working on new systems, and

---

[4] Ibid.

since we the authors are not privy to all the development that is taking place, one could argue that one or more methods might have been left out. If you know of any significant method that is not included in this book, it was accidental and we would like to hear about it so that we could perhaps include it in future editions. Please inform us about other methods by sending e-mail to billk@databased.com or to plenert@aol.com. We would also welcome your comments about the book.

The greatest wasted resource is the human resource.

—WALT DISNEY

Chapter 3

Current and Future Scheduling Advances

What can be worse than being blind?
Having eyes to see, but no vision.
—HELEN KELLER

In the first quarter of 1998 National Semiconductor implemented an FCS dispatching system. With it the company has successfully reduced cycle times and cycle time variations by 50 percent. This has made it more competitive and the facility now runs more consistently.

> We are now much more responsive to our customers' needs, with faster lead times and significantly improved yields.
> —JACQUES MERCIER, corporate manager,
> National Semiconductor

This chapter discusses the development of systems that have supplemented MRP systems to improve capacity management. It also comments on systems that are extensions of MRP—systems like Just-in-Time (JIT), Theory of Constraints (TOC), Demand Flow Manufacturing (DFM), Enterprise Resource Planning (ERP), Supply Chain Management (SCM), and others. The use of these systems will be discussed only briefly and then compared to the integration of MRP and FCS systems.

> The real estate industry claims that three things are important—
> LOCATION, LOCATION, LOCATION.
> In the manufacturing industry the three important things are
> INFORMATION, INFORMATION, INFORMATION.

A Little History

By way of history, we have developed a time line that diagrams the development of production information systems. In Figure 3.1 we see a time line diagramming this development process. We see that prior to World War II (which somewhat marks the advent of computer technology), production scheduling was performed using Economic Order Quantity (EOQ), the two-bin system, and/or linear programming (LP). In the years following World War II, three independent development processes came into use. In the materials-rich United States and Europe, the focus was on MRP systems with an emphasis on labor efficiency. However, in Japan, where labor was abundant but materials, and the financial ability to acquire materials, became the scarce resource, Just-in-Time (JIT) was developed. And in Israel the scarce re-

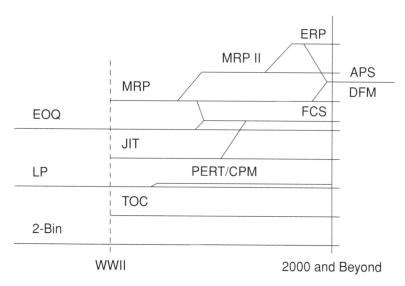

Figure 3.1 Production Scheduling History.

source was capital equipment. Here Theory of Constraints (TOC) was developed with a focus on making the bottleneck machine perform as efficiently as possible.

In time, the three dominant systems found themselves each with their own specialized appropriate environments, depending on which resources factories were attempting to optimize. Either system could turn out to be the best depending on what the factory was trying to accomplish. Factories soon found themselves integrating the systems in an attempt to improve overall performance. For example, most JIT environments in the United States are running within MRP planning environments. Since the two systems focus on optimizing different resources, we find mixed results. In combined MRP-JIT environments we find JIT running at materials efficiency, but at the ends of the JIT production process, where it integrates with the MRP environment, we find that the process is generally stockpiled with inventories to buffer MRP's labor efficiency emphasis.

PERT/CPM (Project Evaluation and Review Technique/Critical Path Methodology) came along offering scheduling in long-term specialized environments like shipbuilding. Both began during the war as manual systems and then were computerized. The U.S. Navy developed PERT, and CPM was developed as a commercial system. These systems were designed for long-term projects and were not meant for manufacturing use. Over time many companies have attempted to apply CPM/PERT to manufacturing with little success. Unfortunately, these tools were not detailed enough to be used for scheduling manufacturing applications; also, maintenance and updating were laborious.

Material Requirements Planning (MRP) evolved into Manufacturing Resources Planning (MRP II), which integrated the manufacturing and the financial management elements of an organization. Later, Enterprise Resource Planning (ERP) became the next stage of evolution and expanded this integration along the supply chain by including engineering, vendors, and distribution into the planning process.

Unfortunately, none of these systems solved the basic problem of offering efficient, capacity-constrained schedules. And that is where FCS offered the ultimate scheduling solution: FCS integrates the planning process of these other manufacturing philosophies with a scheduling process that optimizes on any and all resources, not just a select few.

MATERIAL REQUIREMENTS PLANNING (MRP)

Material Requirements Planning (MRP) systems were designed during an era when labor cost was the highest value-added component in production costs in the United States. Therefore, the focus of MRP was to plan a schedule that made sure that the right materials were in the right place at the right time, thereby maximizing labor efficiency and productivity. Labor is no longer the major factor. Today, in most manufacturing environments material is the highest value-added cost component. This has given the Japanese, with their materials-efficient JIT environment, a competitive edge. Unfortunately, the United States culture has had difficulty separating itself from the feeling that if labor is not busy, then inefficiency exists—when material "is not busy," no one seems to be concerned. FCS eliminates this problem by developing schedules that optimize on all resources, and the system facilitates coordination of materials.

The MRP systems use pegging-files to determine what is required for the next assembly level. However, MRP is not able to determine at what point in time the component parts are required. MRP ensures that parts are available as needed by buffering stock at the work centers at the cost of excess inventory. *Stated simply, MRP defines the where-used function but is not able to manage the when-used function.*

The result of an MRP environment is that schedules are generated through a planning process and then, when it comes time to execute the schedule, the production order is released into the production environment. Production schedules are "pushed" into production, based on an accumulation of lead times. These lead times are based on an average production environment, which rarely, if ever, actually exists. The net effect of this scheduling process can be seen in Figure 3.2. The result is that since we are using average scheduling techniques, then we will also ship goods on time "on the average." Unfortunately, customers want their goods on time every time, not just "on the average."

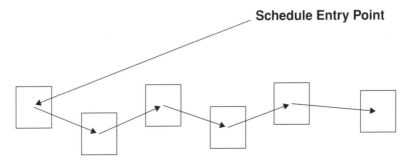

Figure 3.2   The MRP Scheduling Approach.

JUST-IN-TIME (JIT)

There are a number of approaches that have been used to enhance overall productivity, or to help MRP systems enhance productivity. Just-in-Time (JIT) is an example. Although there are some noted exceptions, like the GM Saturn automotive plant or the Numi (New United Motors, Inc.) plant, many will argue, and with some justification, that JIT has not been successful in the United States. In Japan, the JIT approach has worked better than in the Western world, most likely due to cultural differences. Many Western companies did not internalize the JIT philosophy when they incorporated the JIT methodologies.

Material-intensive flow shops have realized more benefits from JIT than have the labor-intensive job shops. In the United States JIT works primarily as a shop floor–administered technique of maintaining material availability and reducing inventory to overcome the MRP system's lack of ability to schedule. JIT functions to supply material as late as possible to minimize inventory but just in time to avoid stopping production; JIT strives to achieve a materials-efficient batch size of one.

The JIT system focuses on minimizing cycle time through minimum inventories. It does this by initiating orders based on a completion schedule. Work in the factory is triggered by a customer order, unlike in MRP where it is triggered by a production schedule based on infinite capacity. The result is that JIT "pulls" schedules through the production process as shown in Figure 3.3.

The emergence of FCS eliminates the need for JIT as a shop floor scheduler for MRP. The FCS system adds functionality beyond JIT by accurately predicting when parts are required. The acronym PJIT (Predictable JIT) is used to describe FCS; PJIT is a massive improvement because it gives the supplier (in-house or outside vendor) advance notice about when each part is going to be needed. This advance notice minimizes the supplier's need to maintain inventory and reduces cost to the manufacturing customer and ultimately to the final consumer.

THEORY OF CONSTRAINTS (TOC)

Theory of Constraints (TOC) is a popular approach for increasing throughput. It is based on Goldratt's approach to managing

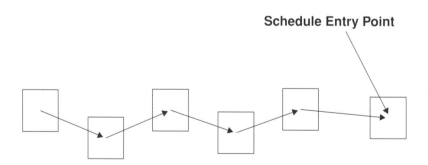

Schedule Entry Point

Figure 3.3   The JIT Scheduling Approach.

capacity by ensuring that the bottleneck work centers always have a queue of work available so that no idle time at the bottleneck will exist. The TOC approach has been successful and has created a large following of devoted users. Much of the success has occurred through manually implemented systems. Moving the concept to computer-based systems causes it to become less definitive; the vendors that have achieved the most success with computer-based TOC systems have added functionality that also schedules the noncritical work centers.

Because TOC focuses on a bottleneck, we find that the entire scheduling process is driven by this bottleneck. Figure 3.4 demonstrates how this scheduling process would operate.

DEMAND FLOW MANUFACTURING (DFM)

John Costanza, chief executive officer (CEO) of John Costanza Institute of Technology, developed the DFM methodology. Its objective is to reduce product cycle time to market. Like JIT and TOC, Demand Flow Manufacturing claims improved throughput over MRP systems.

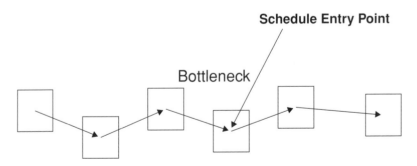

Figure 3.4 The TOC Scheduling Approach.

FINITE CAPACITY SCHEDULING (FCS)

Looking at a diagram of the FCS scheduling process we see that FCS simultaneously schedules all resources and manages all constraints (Figure 3.5). The difference is that FCS schedules are not push, pull, or bottleneck-managed. FCS schedules manage all constraints and flow is maximized across all resources based on available capacity, constraints, and demand. The resulting schedule is realistic and functional.

> [FCS] offered us the constraint-based planning approach and capabilities we were looking for in a mature, "off-the-shelf" product.
>
> —DOMINIC TORIELLO, superintendent, production planning and scheduling, Sparrows Point Division, Bethlehem Steel[1]

Schedule Entry Point

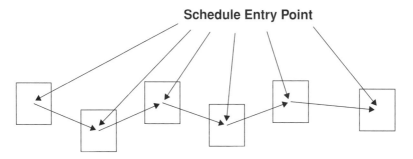

Figure 3.5   The Finite Capacity Scheduling (FCS) Approach.

---

[1] Taken from a presentation by Bethlehem Steel at the 1998 Plant Conference and from a one-page I2 customer case study sheet. RHYTHM is the FCS being referred to.

Bethlehem Steel Corporation is the second largest steel producer in the United States. Its mill is one big bottleneck. If the mill is idle, the company loses money. If they overschedule, the materials are idle and they lose money. Bethlehem Steel needed a tool to coordinate both capacity and materials at all its resources simultaneously. FCS is that tool.

> Our operations run continuously. Jobs must be scheduled precisely so completed orders ship immediately. And we need to make sure our capacity is fully utilized—but not overloaded. . . . We're now able to immediately recognize the dynamics of our operations and use real-time, accurate information to create our plans.
> —Dominic Toriello, superintendent, production planning and scheduling, Sparrows Point Division, Bethlehem Steel[2]

Comparing Production Scheduling Systems

The three system approaches—JIT, TOC, and DFM—are all philosophical concepts that concentrate on a subfunction of the total manufacturing problem. Each of these points to the lack of ability of traditional infinite capacity backward pass scheduling. All of these new scheduling technologies justify their benefit by comparing themselves against MRP's scheduling failures. Since MRP scheduling is bankrupt and always has been, a more realistic analogy would be a

---

[2] Ibid.

comparison based on the other new scheduling approaches. Each of the new systems has its best fit or special niche. Compare them using a common set of data from your application and determine which best fits your needs. Any and all of the systems discussed will win the contest when compared to MRP.

We suggest the term *Modern Scheduling Technology* (MST) as an acceptable term to define and distinguish advanced scheduling methods from traditional scheduling. Next we need to determine how to compare the many new scheduling systems. There is no longer a need for vendors to publish criticism about the inability of MRP to schedule. Vendors and clients will be better served by addressing how to distinguish and compare the more advanced systems.

We would categorize modern scheduling systems into two camps, the first being philosophical approaches and the second being FCS systems. In Chapter 2 we segregated the FCS systems into three different methods, all of which accurately schedule all tasks through all work centers.

Philosophical approaches are designed to concentrate on making a particular resource or function more important than others, while FCS systems allow the user to decide what resources or functions are important and then to develop a model for the application that meets company objectives. This is an important distinction since the philosophical approach is often used as part of a sales presentation. The user should realize that it is more important to do an evaluation based on an actual system performance tested on a level playing field. This is not meant to convey that non-FCS systems are not useful, just that a valid comparison basis should be used for an evaluation to determine what is best for your company.

COMPARING MATERIAL REQUIREMENTS PLANNING (MRP)

The vast majority that read this book will already have an understanding of the purpose, function, and history of MRP. For more detail, see the references for this chapter at the end of this book. For our purposes, an extended discussion on MRP would be redundant. However, some issues need to be addressed in order to demonstrate the value added by modern scheduling technology, particularly FCS systems.

The FCS systems and the various other systems add timely, accurate, and extensive quantities of information beyond the capability provided in MRP systems. The proficiency to assimilate, evaluate, and analyze this production data with a focus on capacity measurement and production management differentiates these systems.

Both MRP and FCS files appear similar in data content; however, a more in-depth evaluation soon exposes the disparity. The systems both contain data about work centers and the total number of workstations available for each shift, and there are numerous other common data fields. So what is the difference? Although the data fields exist, MRP systems have two basic problems that restrict providing the level of details necessary for the accuracy provided by FCS. They are:

1. The assumption of infinite capacity is invalid.

2. Numerous data fields are not available or do not deliver the necessary details.

A discussion of fields missing will demonstrate why MRP is unable to manage capacity. Even if the data fields were included in MRP systems, the infinite capacity assumption would prevent the functionality. The following is a list of some of the data fields or functions missing from MRP systems:

1. Ability to handle multiple resource constraints (the concurrent demand for a machine, a tool, and a setup person is an example).

2. Multilevel setup codes for intermediate setup levels.

3. Move-time fields to manage overlapping tasks and to minimize job cycle time.

4. Partial or multiple resources required for processing an operation.

5. Maximum number of splits that are allowed for a single operation task.

6. First start and last start limits to manage time-critical processes.

7. Ability to specify and select preferred workstations.

These are but a few of the fields missing in MRP systems, and the list goes on. Some will argue that portions of the fields mentioned do exist in some MRP systems, and this is true, but the field is useless if the scheduling functionality is missing.

Consider an MRP system that is integrated with FCS. The MRP system manages all material functions and the FCS system manages all scheduling functions. Information must be shared between the systems; FCS needs to know when material is available to allow jobs to be scheduled, and MRP needs to know when each job is scheduled in order to determine when the material is required. *MRP determines the where-used function and FCS determines the when-used function.*

Since the systems run independent of each other, one system must be run first and then pass the data on to the other system. The obvious question is which should run first. The process is iterative and either can be first. The tradition is to run MRP first; this is not always best. What is desired is to minimize the number of iterations of runs. Our conclusion is that the system that should run first is the system with more constraints. In the real world this is more often the FCS system since most companies have more capacity constraints than material constraints.

The habit of running the material system prior to the capacity system is most likely due to the failure of Capacity Planning System (CPS) within the MRP systems. Prior to the availability of FCS systems, most companies ran only the planning module and the material module and sent a dispatch list to the shop floor. A typical dispatch list contained the jobs, tasks, and due dates but did not sequence the tasks through each work center. Managers on the shop floor actually determined what would run next in each work center. In contrast, FCS systems produce an accurate and detailed work center to-do report that can be followed by shop personnel. Department managers can now manage their departments and not be required to do the scheduling.

MANUFACTURING RESOURCES PLANNING (MRP II)

Manufacturing Resources Planning (MRP II) systems are an expansion of the original MRP environment. Whereas MRP attempted to schedule the production environment in isolation, MRP II attempted to integrate the MRP information set with the accounting processes of an organization. This greatly increased the costing and financial planning functionality of the MRP environment. But MRP II still utilized MRP as the production scheduler. Unfortunately, the additional functionality in MRP II did little to eliminate the capacity management shortcomings of the traditional MRP environments.

ENTERPRISE RESOURCE PLANNING (ERP)

More recently, Enterprise Resource Planning (ERP) systems were introduced as another evolutionary step in the MRP II chain of development, adding functionality to allow for integration of vendors, customers, and distributors into the MRP II information network. This initiated the roots of what is now known as Supply Chain Management (SCM).

A good place to start in defining ERP is to use the APICS definition:

Enterprise Resource Planning (ERP) system
1. An accounting-oriented information system for identifying and planning the enterprisewide resources needed to take, make, ship and account for customer orders. An ERP system differs from the typical MRP system in technical requirements such as graphical language and computer-assisted software engineering tools in development, client/server architecture and open system portability.

81

2. More generally, a method for the effective planning and control of all resources needed to take, make, ship and account for customer orders in a manufacturing, or service company.[3]

Most often, MRP systems managed plants that were autonomous of other plants or divisions of the company, while ERP implies a coordination of multiple plants (i.e., managing the entire enterprise). This coordination naturally requires coordination of vendors and customers. Note also that no reference is made to scheduling in the APICS definition of ERP, only to planning.

The prevailing conditions influencing the move to ERP are the rapid advancements in communication, information technology, transportation, and consolidation of multinational companies and/or suppliers throughout the world. The major motivating factor is shorter product cycle time, thereby improving time-to-market.

The term ERP does not have rigid boundaries. Software vendors tend to define ERP by the applications they offer and often by specific industries; there is no standard list of applications. There is also an implication that an ERP system manages resources beyond a company's resources, one example being management of distribution. Although ERP is represented as focusing on the management of resources throughout the enterprise, it is difficult at the writing of this book to find ERP systems with short interval scheduling solutions. Something is wrong with this picture.

---

[3] Taken from *APICS Dictionary*, 9th ed., Falls Church, VA: APICS, 1998, p. 30.

What is more important than managing the resources that add value to products manufactured by the enterprise? Why has short interval scheduling been left out of ERP systems until recently?

We have already established that short interval scheduling has been ignored by MRP, which cannot cope with the dynamics of the shop floor, being based on fixed lead times, predetermined batch sizes, and safety stock. These conditions do not represent shop floor reality. To a large degree this same approach exists in ERP since ERP is an exterior expansion of MRP rather than any type of structural change to the processes. Generally, ERP vendors seem to ignore completely the process of scheduling production and default to the same standard lead times. Some ERP vendors establish fixed product cycle time through each plant based on predetermined conditions.

How are ERP vendors planning to solve the short interval scheduling problem? Most vendors have by now acknowledged this need and are in the process of creating a solution. A number of ERP vendors have purchased or partnered with independent FCS vendors in order to deliver scheduling capabilities. We believe this trend will continue because of the time and expense required to develop a capable FCS.

In general, ERP vendors have been successful without the scheduling module because clients have been able to realize enough improvement by using the added ERP features without being concerned with short interval scheduling. As continued competitive improvements become more difficult to find, the scheduling application will have to be addressed.

ERP stands for *enterprise resource planning.*
But what does it mean? There are as many
answers to that question as there are ERP
software vendors. Of course, there is plenty
of overlap between the different vendor
and consultant definitions, but there is
substantially less agreement between
vendors (singly and as a whole) and the
manufacturing professionals who pay for
the systems.

Those end-users—who cross their fingers
and forgo sleep during implementation—
often scratch their heads when their
bottom-line results don't match their
expectations. Usually it's because of
differing definitions of specific
functionality promised by salespeople or
sales materials. Vendors need to begin
defining their systems in terms of
functionality, rather than relying on
acronyms.

—Gregory A. Farley, *APICS—The
Performance Advantage*, March 1998

The following are two concepts of how an ERP system
can be implemented. Figure 3.6 is a configuration that imple-
ments ERP as a true multiplant, multidivision, or multinational company. This approach defines a completely
integrated management system, including all the divisions or
companies involved in the enterprise.

A potential problem with this approach is that estimated lead times are used for product cycle times through
each plant. Cycle times for ERP, like MRP queue times, are

not consistent; they vary with demand, order mix, and other conditions.

Figure 3.6 represents a company that manufactures products in a multiplant operation. This company model builds component parts in plants A and B and the final product is manufactured and assembled in plant N. The company delivers the final assembly to customers from plant N. Plant A manufactures subassemblies that are shipped to plant B and to outside customers. Plant B manufactures subassemblies that are shipped to plant N and to outside clients. In this concept, the planning is at a high level, uses estimated product cycle times, and does not consider short interval scheduling.

The vertical product structure of Figure 3.6 is quite common for many large companies with some divisions shipping products to other divisions and also shipping products to outside customers from each division. The ratio of products that go to outside customers compared to the

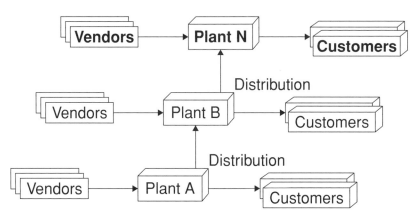

Figure 3.6 The Enterprise.

internal company will have implications as to which customer gets the higher priority when conflicts occur. If a large majority of a division's production supports the parent company's products, then the division will be heavily influenced by corporate. If, however, the majority of a division's output is to outside customers, the division president will have a responsibility for profits, and conflicts in customer priority will reflect a different conviction. This type of problem is prevalent in multidivisional and multinational companies that have both vertical integration and a high ratio of product deliveries to outside customers. The second case demands better scheduling to manage resources and resolve conflicts.

An alternative ERP approach that reduces control from a central system and distributes more responsibility to the individual plants is described in Figure 3.7. This plan suggests more autonomy at each plant and requires a good

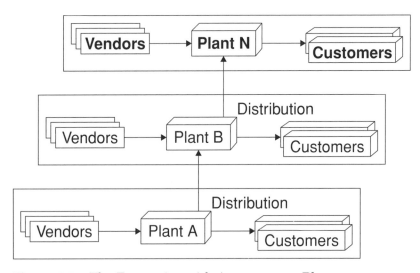

Figure 3.7   The Enterprise with Autonomous Plants.

communication network. This configuration will be a better alternative for many companies. Autonomy at each plant does not imply that the corporate business plan needs to change.

However, this book is about modern scheduling technology, not about ERP. These two ERP scenarios are simply used to create a format for discussing the enterprise and to highlight the importance of resource utilization, particularly when conflicting management circumstances are prevalent.

BEYOND ERP

Companies make profits by adding value. This implies maximizing the utilization of resources at every level. The manufacturing process is a major point where value is added, and effectively managing capacity is the key. That is what FCS is all about.

In its September 1998 issue, *Industry Week* published an interview with Peter Drucker. Mr. Drucker suggests that conditions in the manufacturing sector are becoming blurred with the service sector. He introduces the concept of "the systematic process of production," which includes traditional manufacturing of "things" and the creation of "intangibles" such as software or services. In the article, Mr. Drucker states:

> If we redefine manufacturing as "the systematic process of production," manufacturing is indeed the most important part of any world-class economy. . . . The most important technical change in the last 30 or 40 years is that of the process of production, first developed in traditional manufacturing and now embracing more and

more of the economy. It is becoming the process of production. It does not necessarily produce goods. But the new goods—still usually classified as "services"—increasingly are being organized on the principles of production that were first developed in manufacturing.

The trend suggested by the article is that although the manufacturing of "things" continues to increase, the ratio of "things" to "services" is getting smaller. This trend indicates that software designed for manufacturing companies will also be beneficial to service companies.

The trend toward the increasing service industry is important to manufacturing software vendors because a larger market will be available for their products. The service industry will be somewhat different in that the importance of material management will diminish and the importance of capacity management will increase. This will gain the attention of ERP vendors, forcing them to realize that the traditional MRP approach of crudely estimating cycle times will not bode well in the future. This trend in fact could develop a market in favor of Advanced Planning and Scheduling (APS) vendors, since the demand for material control will not be as significant. Many of these service companies will have little or no material to manage.

Why has the inclusion of modern scheduling technology in MRP/ERP systems been delayed so long? One reason is because scheduling is the most difficult application to manage in manufacturing and is even more difficult in an enterprise environment. The MRP vendors basically ignored the problem until recently and still do not appear to have a clear understanding of how to deal with the capacity issues. Because it is difficult is no reason to ignore the problem.

Figure 3.7 suggested a looser connection in the management of the enterprise supply chain to allow for improved production efficiency at each plant. This approach specifically includes short interval scheduling at each plant to eliminate the need for fixed product lead times. Scheduling would be autonomous at each plant and the output to other plants would be accessed from the enterprise-wide database.

The MRP/ERP a company chooses to implement would be dependent on many variables. The first approach (Figure 3.6) would fit vertical product companies with more predictable flow-oriented products, and the second approach (Figure 3.7) is more for companies that have a varied order mix and external customers.

Some individuals will argue that FCS systems assume infinite material availability. This is true. Most FCS systems assume material will be available as required. However, FCS systems are designed to obtain actual material availability from the MRP system. When the MRP system passes data to the FCS system advising it that material is not available as scheduled, then, upon rescheduling, the FCS system will delay the release date (i.e., delay the start date) until the material is available as reported by the MRP system. This is how MRP and FCS combine to form an iterative team solution.

ADVANCED PLANNING AND SCHEDULING (APS)

Advanced Planning and Scheduling (APS) systems are emerging. Most vendors that currently identify their systems as APS systems previously identified those systems as FCS. The approach that these vendors use for scheduling in what is now referred to as APS is the same approach that was applied in their earlier FCS system. However, additional application functions have been added, in some cases including a material system.

The planning and scheduling functionality within APS systems was well established as part of FCS long before APS appeared. The transition to new terminology from FCS to APS was helped by the early resistance to FCS by MRP vendors and users. Although they are referred to as APS systems, Finite Capacity Scheduling (FCS) methodologies predominate as the basis for scheduling.

The designation of APS is an appropriate distinction since APS vendors are offering application modules to supplement the FCS planning and scheduling functions. Vendors vary in which application modules are offered to supplement the scheduling function. Some of the applications supported are:

- Material.
- Forecasting.
- Distribution.
- Transportation.

These additional application modules are what distinguish and enhance APS systems beyond the foundation FCS systems.

Supply Chain Management (SCM)

Another currently popular term that deserves mention is Supply Chain Management (SCM). The distinction between SCM and ERP is difficult. They both are evolving to manage multiple levels of the enterprise. A distinction that generally applies is that ERP evolved from MRP through MRP II: MRP is the production planning process, MRP II applies the accounting information integration, and ERP enhances this by introducing engineering information integration and multi-site integration. This allows engineering information to be passed from our customers to our engineers, and to terminals on the production floor. These same drawings can also be passed to other facilities within an organization or to vendors. Most of the information transfer occurs through some form of e-commerce technology utilizing intranet or Internet systems.

The SCM systems take ERP integration to the next level. With SCM, there is engineering technology and scheduling data interchange linking the vendor's vendor through to the customer's customer. Customers are able to check on the delivery performance of our vendors. Advanced systems allow customers to check their job on the vendor's production floor. They can use e-mail to place orders and receive scheduling commitments for deliveries. The integration of this supply chain offers customer competitiveness by shrinking the total start-to-finish cycle time of all steps in the procurement and manufacturing process. And because of the feedback and real-time responsiveness of this system, it offers customers the ability to monitor and to some extent even control their own schedules, based on when they place orders into the production planning system.

CONCLUSION

Often the distinctive difference in manufacturing software is with the functional applications. Vendor capabilities vary greatly at these different levels. For example, a prospect may prefer vendor A's financial systems and vendor B's scheduling and distribution systems. No vendor is a best fit for all applications. Therefore, selecting which vendor is best for your company is a difficult and complex task. It is usually a trade-off of identifying which are the most important functions for your company. This tends to force a selection of software based on the more critical functions.

Software development that is taking place in the manufacturing sector is progressing so rapidly that specific conditions and statements made during the writing of this book may be somewhat out of date by the time the book is published. However, the broad-based direction should remain valid for some time.

At the rate we learnin' these things we won't know nothin' in no time.
—BOLDER, BRISCO COUNTY JR.

Chapter 4

The Selection of a Scheduling Methodology

The towers of tomorrow are built upon
the foundations of today.
—Alfred Lord Tennyson

The purpose of this book is to turn production technology upside down. We'll start by setting up 10 bowling pins, as shown in Figure 4.1. The objective is to turn the triangle formed by these 10 pins upside down. We want the 10 pins to form a new triangle, but this time pointing downward. We want to get them into this position by moving only three of the pins. Can you do it? If you can, then you're on your way.

> **Where you are in life isn't nearly as important**
> **as in what direction you're going.**

Figure 4.1 Ten Bowling Pins.

In the first quarter of 1998 a real-time dispatching FCS system was implemented at Macronix International, Co., Ltd., a wafer manufacturer in Taiwan, R.O.C. Today, 90 percent of the tools utilize FCS scheduling methods. As a result, the company has experienced cycle time reductions of 31.3 percent and a 52.3 percent reduction in cycle time deviation. But most importantly, it has experienced the trust and total acceptance of the FCS scheduling process by its operators.[1]

OVERVIEW

This chapter reviews the procedure for selecting a scheduling method and the additional considerations for selecting an FCS system. What are needed (setting scheduling objectives

---

[1] "Real Time Dispatching System Delivers Dramatic Cycle Time Reductions at Macronix," a working paper by Ying-Jen Chen, Yeaun-Jyn Su, Ming-Shing Hong, and Ivan Wang.

and defining the outputs)? What is necessary for success (defining features and functions)? How should it function (identifying the process)? How do you search out the best system? How do you make a system selection? What is the best process for implementation? What are some critical considerations?

SELECTING A SCHEDULING SYSTEM

Chapter 3 discussed the types of manufacturing systems that are currently available. It briefly described the scheduling functionality—or lack thereof—of each of the systems. The value of a manufacturing software system is the sum of its overall effectiveness. Overall effectiveness is a function of the effectiveness of each subsystem. Manufacturing management systems are like a chain; a weak link restricts overall effectiveness. Scheduling, for most organizations, is currently a weak link. This chapter will address the issues involved with selecting the scheduling application in order to strengthen the total system.

Understanding the scheduling methods defined in Chapter 2 is the first step in selecting a scheduling system. Once a system has been selected you are stuck with it. The method of calculation of the selected system is not likely to change, however new features will be added over time. There is not a universal best choice for any specific application type. There are too many supplementary factors that need to be considered—for example, to focus selection on the critical resource, or the culture of the organization.

A major consideration in selecting the scheduling method involves the management style of the company. We define scheduling management as having a broad spectrum with a strategic approach at one end of the spectrum and a tactical approach at the other end. Many combinations of strategic and tactical options exist between the two extremes. Some companies operate on the basis of being highly customer service oriented, toward the tactical end. Other companies tend to operate with a more strategic approach. Some management styles are highly participatory and emphasize information sharing while others are more authoritarian and controlling. Where your company fits within this spectrum must be influential in selecting a vendor.

The number of variables that need to be considered is enormous, so making a rigid statement about where the methods fit is not appropriate. In general, the job-based method is more adapted to service-oriented companies that use a hands-on approach and desire to make frequent adjustments to the schedule. The event-based method is more adapted to strategic management and is appropriate for companies that prefer to maximize throughput and minimize tactical decisions as much as possible. However, either management style is capable of operating at either end of the spectrum. The trade-offs are often subtle but important.

C.J. McNair and Richard Vangermeersch in their book *Total Capacity Management* offer a valuable insight into capacity management as it relates to the strategic and tactical management of capacity. They segregate what we refer to as tactical into tactical and operational. (Although we have often seen operational grouped with the tactical camp, the separation of the two is a preferred way of viewing the changing time frames.)

Table 4.1, from *Total Capacity Management*, describes the three time frames for managing capacity in the typical cycle of a company. The time frames each represent management control at different levels.

Table 4.1 Capacity Cost Management Phases

	Time Frame of Analysis		
	Short-Term	Intermediate-Term	Long-Term
Value chain emphasis	Velocity through existing processes	Removing NVA (non-value-added) activities from processes	Structural changes
Range of motion	Highly constrained	Moderate constraints	Minimal constraints
Management level involved	Lower to middle	All levels	Top management

Source: C.J. McNair and Richard Vangermeersch, *Total Capacity Management*, Boca Raton, FL: St. Lucie Press, 1998.

Strategic level decisions will be the responsibility of upper management. These decisions deal with the long-term direction and policies of the company. Constructing the FCS model will be based on these strategic decisions. Once the fundamental FCS model is built, management can enter various conditions (i.e., modify parameters) and perform what-if analysis. In minutes management can see the effect of modified environmental factors.

The time frame for modifying a company's strategy will vary greatly and will be influenced by the products being produced. Companies that are manufacturing capital equipment with product cycle times of six months or more will have longer lead times for the revision of strategic plans than a company with one-week product cycle times. When management revises strategy, it is necessary to revise the FCS model to reflect the revisions.

The book *Total Capacity Management* defines the three time frames as:

> The strategic time frame allows for questioning and changing all physical, product-driven, and process-based constraints of the existing system.

> Intermediate-term, tactical time frames are where management decisions on capacity emphasize the changes in the processes that make up the value chain.

> Short-term, operational time frames are where decisions are focused on the flow of resources through existing plant and processes.[2]

We have reversed the order as presented to correspond with the flow of data for developing an FCS model.

A major benefit of a computer-based FCS system is that it delivers a high level of instant and accurate communication throughout the company. Each reschedule delivers an immediate update to all departments including a detailed sequence of tasks through every work center (WC). Compare this immediate updating and revision of sequencing at each work center to a traditional MRP system that delivers dispatch lists with job and due date and no detailed sequences at each work center. The dynamic scheduling system coordinates all departments to maximize performance of the company strategy. The traditional MRP approach requires each department to make decisions in-

---

[2] Taken from the book by C.J. McNair and Richard Vangermeersch entitled *Total Capacity Management* (IMA Foundation for Applied Research, Inc.), Boca Raton, FL: St. Lucie Press, 1998.

dependently, which often conflict with other departments' decisions.

A decision to make a change on the shop floor with an MRP dispatch list would require a verbal exchange to be passed up and down between management levels. This production change most often causes a change in other departments, which in turn requires the verbal transmission of information. Communication under this mode of operation is slow and disruptive. With FCS, all details are available to all parties each time a new schedule is created, resulting in more stability and less frequent rescheduling.

Tactical (intermediate-term) decisions are usually made by middle management. At this level, adjustments to the schedule are due to any number of conditions that can occur—for example, changes in customer orders, process problems, or machine failure.

Some decisions at the short-term, operational time frame can be made within a single department without triggering the need to reschedule. However, a condition like the failure and loss of a major resource for a significant period of time will affect downstream production. This type of change will trigger rescheduling. With FCS the rescheduling will adjust all WCs based on the loss of capacity, and the new schedule will communicate details to all the affected areas immediately upon updating the new schedule.

What is necessary for success (defining features and functions)?

The most important factor that will ensure success in choosing a scheduling system is to make certain that all the features and functions you require are included in a scripted demo. It is best to minimize the work required by creating a subset of data that represents all of the difficult scheduling problems associated with your application. It is not necessary to include all work centers and all routings contained in your application. A subset of data that tests each of the required features and functions is adequate. This then becomes the test data. Tables 4.2, 4.3, and 4.4 are formatted examples of work center, routing, and job file data. The WC or resource file will contain all the information about each work center, including the number of resources available on each shift.

These three files contain a high percentage of the total data needed for a scripted demo. If additional constraint information needs to be considered, it can be supplied in the form of text specifications.

Testing the data is another challenge. Do not expect to take routings from your MRP files and think that you have the data required for a scripted demo. The MRP files do not include all of the files or the level of detail that is necessary to test FCS systems. To ensure that the data is complete and accurate, the data needs to be processed through a scheduling engine to make certain all constraints are met and that all inconsistencies or unfeasible data are eliminated. Clients may need consulting assistance to ensure that the data is comprehensive and comparable for all vendors.

When the data is fully developed and tested, a good method for delivering the data to vendors is by using a spreadsheet format. Vendors can download the data from the spreadsheet into a format acceptable to their specific FCS system. We have repeatedly used this method and received good results. If any inconsistency exists in the data, vendors will be quick to advise of the problem and the error can then be corrected for all participating vendors.

Finally getting to the all-important systems features and functions, we will list only some of the most used features. The list will obviously not include all possibilities for all

Table 4.2 Example of the Work Center or Resource File

Work Center ID	Work Center Name	Shifts per Day	Total Number of Resources	Resources on Shift 1	Resources on Shift 2	Resources on Shift 3
Cut	Cut	3	5	5	5	5
Drill	Drill	3	3	3	2	0
Shear	Shear	2	3	2	1	0
OV-HT	Outside Vendor Heat Treat	1	1	1	1	1
MA-A	Module A Assembly	1	1	1	1	1
Test	Testing	1	2	2	0	0

Table 4.3 Example of the Routing File

Routing ID	Sequence #	WC ID	Task Description	Resources Required	Setup Time	Time per Unit	Maximum Split	Move Time	Quantity Multiple
AG-4182	100	Cut	Cut per drawing #	1	0.25	2.50	1	0	20
	110	Shear	Shear	1	0.10	1.75	1	0	20
	120	Drill	Drill	1	0.00	3.00	1	0	10
	130	MA-A	Assembly	2	10.00	22.00	1	0	10

Table 4.4 Example of Job File

Customer ID	Job #	Assemble into Job #	Routing ID	Job Quantity	Job Priority	Job Release Date-Time	Job Due Date-Time
CUS1	JOB1		D0100	5	Default	09/10/98-00:00	09/14/98-23:59
CUS3	JOB2		128	1	Default	09/11/98-08:15	09/15/98-23:59
CUS5	JOB3		AG-4182	100	Default	09/11/98-00:00	09/19/98-23:59
CUS11	JOB4		134	1	Default	09/12/98-00:00	09/13/98-23:59
CUS2	JOB5		142	3	2	09/11/98-01:40	09/14/98-23:59
CUS3	JOB6	JOB2	126	1	1	09/11/98-00:00	09/15/98-23:59
CUS1	JOB7		122	2	3	09/14/98-00:00	09/16/98-23:59

prospective buyers. It will, however, include features customarily used by most companies, regardless of the types of user applications or products being produced or services being rendered. The terms for defining features and functions will vary by vendors; however, the functionality expressed by each vendor is explicit and the interpretation is generally obvious.

FEATURES AND FUNCTIONS

The features discussed in this section are pertinent to all scheduling methods. However, vendors have their own methods of implementing the various features and the different techniques will produce varying results, all vendors will argue that their method is best. Once a vendor selects a scheduling method, the method chosen will exert some limitations on the system functionality. Conversely, the method selected will offer a performance advantage in other areas of system functionality. Whether the vendor-selected method contributes to or restricts the performance of the process will vary depending on the features selected.

Features can also conflict with each other. As an example, if a setup minimization function overrides other conditions in order to reduce setup, some jobs may suffer by missing the promised due dates. It is obviously desirable to reduce setup. However, where do you draw the line when reducing setup causes some jobs to be late?

Many additional conflicts exist with any complex scheduling application. This brings us back to the importance of modeling the scheduling system to support the strategic plan of the company where trade-offs are inevitable. Understand that the scheduling vendor will offer an array of tools (features and functions) and the user will have a great deal of autonomy in how to make use of a large number of options. The number of options makes user decisions extremely important. These user decisions are more important when modeling a scheduling application than for most other software implementation decisions. Since you are emulating the schedule prior to actually implementing the schedule, the user has the ability an opportunity to make changes when results are not acceptable. Training and practice are necessary in order to make effective modeling decisions.

The features we have chosen to discuss have been selected because they are common to many applications. This is a small set of the total features possible in the universe. No vendor will have all possible features, and vendor implementation of features will vary dramatically.

The first features we will be discussing are move-time conditions, that is, sequencing of tasks within jobs. This feature is predominantly about the relationship of previous and following tasks and the control of when a following task is allowed to begin relative to its predecessor. The default condition for most vendor systems is a sequential move time that restricts a following task from processing until the previous task has completed processing. We will define a total of five move-time conditions, each of which can contribute to increasing throughput. Each move-time function should be optional and user-controlled.

The five move-time relationships are exhibited in Figures 4.2 through 4.6. Vendors' terminology will differ, but the functionally is what is important, regardless of the specific terms being used. To simplify the graphic presentation, the move-time relationships depicted in Figures 4.2 through 4.6 assume that no queuing constraints exist (i.e., that a resource is always available to process the task as shown in the

104

graphic). This is not true in a real application. Some tasks will be queued and the scheduling system would have to account for the competition and delay operations until a resource is available to process the task in question. This becomes yet another complexity in developing a generic scheduling system for multiple users.

Our description starts with the sequential relationship as depicted in Figure 4.2. In this example, three tasks make up a job and each task (operation) must complete processing prior to starting the next operation.

Figure 4.3 depicts a positive move-time condition such that a following task cannot begin until some specified time after the previous task has completed processing. The traditional example of a positive move-time situation is the time needed to move a job from one work center to the next. Modern scheduling systems offer additional positive move-time options for more control. Examples of other positive move-time situations would be to allow time for paint to

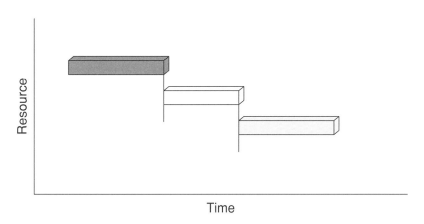

Figure 4.2   Sequential Move-Time Relationship.

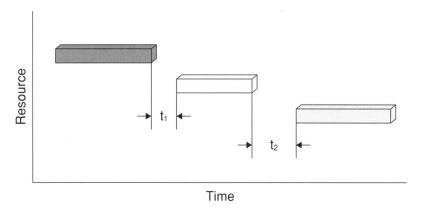

Figure 4.3 Positive Move-Time Relationship.

dry, time for a chemical process to take place, or time for metal to cool.

A positive move-time situation implies that no resource is required during the move time. If, for instance, drying paint requires a conveyor to pass the painted objects through a heated oven, this would not be a move-time relationship because a resource would be required for the process to take place. This process would be specified as an operation requiring time in the oven and possibly a hook on a conveyor.

Figure 4.4 shows an overlapping relationship that allows for a following task to begin prior to finishing a previous task. This overlapping condition can exist only when the quantity is equal to or greater than two units. Systems that allow tasks to overlap operations contribute greatly to reducing cycle time. Overlapping is probably the single most important factor in reducing cycle time. Note that if the process time for the following task is greater than for the previous task, the following task can begin as soon as the first unit of the previous task has finished processing. If the following task's process time is less than that of the previous task, then a calculation must determine the earliest possible start for the following task in order to avoid starts and stops for the following task.

Figure 4.5 depicts concurrent processing of multiple tasks within a single job. This implies that independent operations

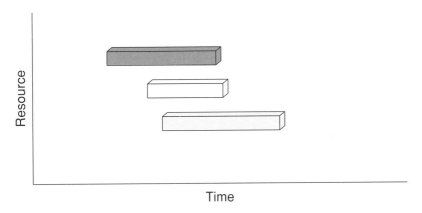

Figure 4.4   Overlapping Tasks.

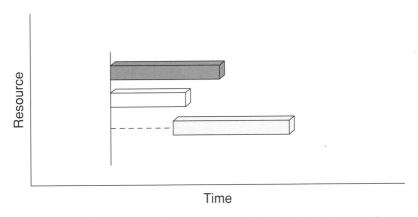

Figure 4.5   Concurrent Operations with One Task Queued.

can process concurrently. In the example, the last (bottom) task is queued while the previous tasks are being processed. This move-time relationship is not used very often but needs to be noted as a possible option.

Figure 4.6 shows an operation that requires multiple resources simultaneously in order for the operation to proceed. Case 1 of this example depicts the need for an operator, a tool, and a machine. If any of the three resources are missing, the operation is delayed until such time when all resources are available.

Case 2 depicts a similar example requiring the same three resources; however, the operator is required only for the setup (S/U). Upon completion of setup the operator is available to process the next task in the queue.

Figure 4.7 demonstrates a method to calibrate and report the Q-ratio of jobs. (Q-ratio equals cycle time divided by work content.) A Q-ratio value of 1 indicates the job has no idle time. High values for Q-ratios mean excessive idle time and are obviously undesirable. Idle time increases cycle time,

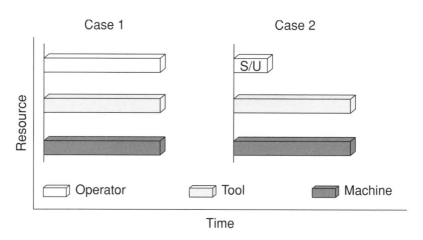

Figure 4.6 Multiple Resource Constraints.

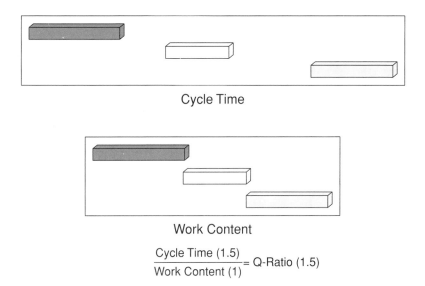

Cycle Time

Work Content

$$\frac{\text{Cycle Time (1.5)}}{\text{Work Content (1)}} = \text{Q-Ratio (1.5)}$$

Figure 4.7   Q-Ratio.

work in progress (WIP), and shop floor clutter. It is important to note that Q-ratio values can be less than 1 if the overlapping of tasks is performed.

Q-ratio is a simple calculation and should be monitored as a measure of excessive cycle times. Figure 4.7 displays the Q-ratio showing the cycle time and the work content of a hypothetical job with a Q-ratio of 1.5.

Figure 4.8 depicts a condition of assigning more than a single workstation to the task if multiple workstations are available and the production quantity justifies extra resources. Multiple workstations will complete the job in a shorter time than a single workstation. However, if setup time is required and is significant, the resultant setup may eliminate the benefit of using multiple workstations. This is a condition that requires the scheduling system to make complex

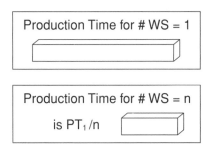

Figure 4.8   Splitting Tasks to Utilize Multiple Resources for a Single Operation, Assuming No Setup Is Required.

decisions during the scheduling process. The first question is whether multiple workstations are available. Next we ask what effect on tying up two or more WS for the task in question has on other tasks in the queue, if a queue exists, and what the setup conditions are for the job. Modeling decisions by the user will play an important part in determining when multiple resources are applied.

Figures 4.2 through 4.8 have demonstrated time-dependent decisions during scheduling. The scheduling system must be capable of making decisions that maintain high throughput, high utilization of resources, and minimized lateness. These are real-life and conflicting conditions. In the JobTime Plus system we allowed for multiple resource limitations to be set by the operator for any task. The operator could specify that multiple resources would be allowed. However, this feature should limit the number to no more than n workstations for this specific task, leaving all other workstations available for other tasks in the queue.

This complexity becomes great when considering just this example of a single decision point, and there are many alternate decisions possible each time a task arrives at a work center to be processed. This accentuates the degree of complexity and the enormous number of combinations and permutations that are possible and that must be considered during scheduling such that no constraint is violated and a feasible solution is achieved.

The time required to process a task using multiple workstations is shown in Figure 4.8; the system must not exceed the number of workstations available.

Setup minimization is one of the most important functions if your application has a need for minimizing setups. When one or more resources offer the opportunity to reduce setup by selectively aligning identical or similar operations, the reduction in total workload at that resource can be enormous.

The approaches used by vendors to implement setup minimization will likely be different for every vendor, and the range of effectiveness will also be extreme. This feature, if appropriate for your application, should receive dedicated evaluation to determine if the vendor of choice includes the capability of managing resources that require changeover. Some vendor solutions only match identical setups; others offer some degree of partial setup matching, and the very capable vendors offer a high degree of setup minimization based on a user-defined matrix of varying conditions.

Figures 4.9A and 4.9B depict a generic setup example that allows for setup reduction during changeover for a series of operations through a single workstation. The time required for changeover at the resource varies depending on the degree of match between the setups when moving from a previous to a following task. Figure 4.9A shows the sequence of operations without considering the possibility of setup

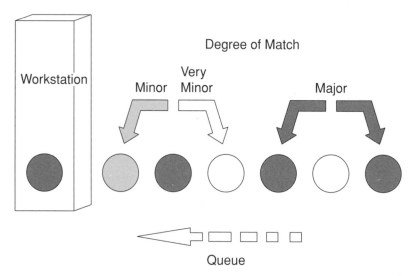

Figure 4.9A Primary Schedule.

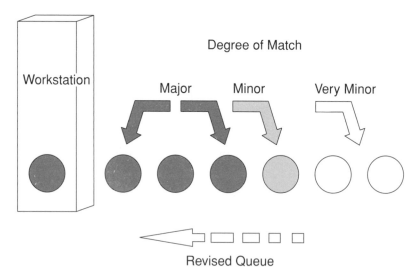

Figure 4.9B Setup Override Schedule.

minimization. In this example, each task would require its full setup allotment.

Figure 4.9B shows how the tasks would be sequenced to take advantage of logic for minimizing changeovers. The system automatically realigns the tasks to minimize setup. Three different levels of setup reduction are exhibited. The first is a major setup condition such that the following task is identical to the previous task and requires no setup. The second is a minor setup condition such that the following task is similar but not identical to the previous task and requires some percent of the total setup; the third is a very minor setup such that the following task requires another incremental setup.

The user is required to define all of the possible setup variables and times. These conditions are then applied to the vendor system. Clients should thoroughly investigate vendor techniques when setup minimization is a scheduling requirement to ensure getting an effective system for the application.

This is a very brief discussion of setup minimization. To adequately describe setup minimization would require an entire second book dedicated completely to the subject. Some industries have controlling factors that make it exceedingly difficult to select the setup sequence and to ensure that the selected sequence is the best choice. Bill Kirchmier worked on a dye application with a company in the fabrics industry. The application involved setup reduction not only for color selection but also for a choice of two different roll widths for the same operation. Other conflicting factors were also involved that impacted the setup sequence. This application had hundreds of orders, each with a due date that also required consideration.

The FCS scheduling engine was able to perform

substantially better than the company's conventional approach. However, getting a critical mass of management and personnel on the side of new technology proved impossible and the system was ultimately dropped. This example, like other failures, is a warning that a successful application requires both an understanding of the technology and the support of company personnel—not only management but also personnel involved in the process.

The vendors' plant calendar will typically define the number of shifts by day of the week for each work center and the number of resources for each shift. *Variable capacity over time* is a feature that allows the user to change work center capacity at the shift level for specific future dates or a range of dates. This short-term alteration option is used to adjust capacity to reflect such variables as vacations, maintenance downtime, and overtime schedules to meet short-term demand.

Table 4.5 shows an example of using the variable capacity over time feature to adjust the work center capacity for maintenance downtime. Normal conditions for the work center are a pattern of four resources for two shifts as shown by conditions on 7/14/98. On 7/20/98 a resource is to be down for maintenance until 7/28/98. When the resource is sched-

Table 4.5 Variable Capacity over Time—
Adjusting for Maintenance Downtime

Date	Shift 1	Shift 2	Shift 3
7/14/98	4	4	0
7/20/98	3	3	1
7/28/98	4	4	0

uled for downtime on 7/20/98, the scheduling system responds to the maintenance plan, and to compensate for the loss of capacity due to the downtime it adds a third shift for one machine. The work center reverts back to the normal shift pattern on 7/28/98.

Figure 4.10 is an example of a work center that contains dissimilar resources. The variable in the example is the size of shaft that can be turned on a lathe. In this case four lathes with size varying from two inches to six inches are usable as shown in Figure 4.10. The objective is to use the lathe that is best suited for the task, but if the preferred resource is not available then to select the next preferred option that is available.

In this example two operations are shown. The operation of task 1 is limited to using only resource A or B with B as the preferred resource. Task 2 is a shaft of size two inches or less and the preferred resource is either C or D. However, the selection criterion allows for option B or A if neither C nor D is available. As with all features, vendors will have

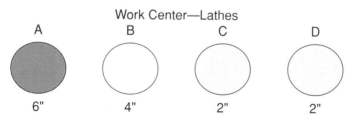

Task 1—Select WS B, then A.
Task 2—Select WS C or D, then B, then A.
Default — Select any WS available.

Figure 4.10 Preferred Workstations.

their own method of managing this condition for selecting the preferred resource.

Some vendors separate the different size resources into multiple work centers and use an alternate work center approach rather than a preferred workstation approach. This practice conforms to the traditional MRP approach. Some vendors may offer both options.

Figure 4.11 depicts an example of variable shift patterns for work centers. This is a very typical condition in many companies. Engineering may work only on shift 1 and the plant may run two or three shifts. The scheduling system needs to accommodate all of the variable patterns necessary to model the company's application. This example shows three different shift pattern options. The user should be able to specify as many patterns as are needed and assign the patterns to work centers as appropriate. A variable number of hours per shift is also an option.

The previous features have been examples of task-oriented functionality. Two important job-oriented features will follow, and there are many additional possibilities be-

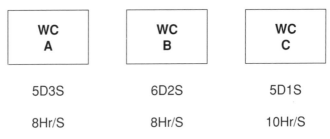

Unique Calendar for Each Work Center

Figure 4.11 Variable Shift Patterns.

yond these two examples. The objective is to demonstrate that many possibilities exist, and few, if any, vendors will have them all. It is important to match the vendor to the features you need.

The standard convention used by MRP systems for managing assembly relationship functionality is to build subassemblies and consider them as stock. When the next assembly level requires subassemblies they are retrieved from stock and the material level is adjusted.

The FCS systems can determine when the subassemblies are needed and then coordinate the production process for all subassemblies, as shown in Figure 4.12. This eliminates the necessity of moving or pretending to move the parts to and from stock. The FCS system will not start production on subassemblies until they can be scheduled to arrive as needed. FCS will coordinate the timing of each subassembly with its

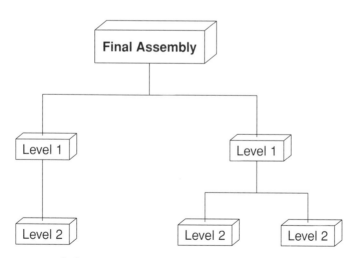

Figure 4.12 Subassembly Relationship.

assembly level. Small parts that do not represent high dollar value may be built independently as batch jobs and stocked as required. Ensure that the software vendor's number of subassembly levels is sufficient for your application.

Assembly jobs have a comparable inverted state, albeit not as frequently required, as the subassembly-to-assembly relationship does. However, the relationship is indispensable when needed. We call this inverted condition a "batch lot" relationship. Figure 4.13 uses the example of mixing a batch of cereal and concurrently packaging the cereal into three different size boxes on three different packaging lines. The cereal batch must be fully blended before processing on any of the three packaging lines. The amount (weight or volume) of cereal to be packaged in each size also needs to be managed by the scheduling engine. This would typically be managed by specifying the quantity (weight or volume) of each lot job. It is also expedient to use a consistency check for the scheduling

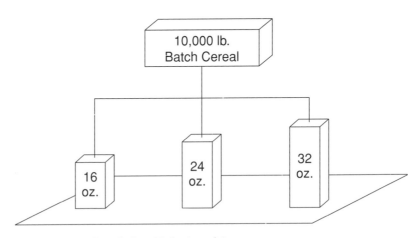

Figure 4.13   Batch Lot Relationship.

engine to confirm that the sum of the lots is equal to the batch lot quantity.

FUTURE FCS OPTIONS

What does the future of FCS have to offer? The past 15 years of FCS development have seen computation speeds go from 10 to 20 computations per minute in 1985 to thousands of tasks per minute today. Speed in the beginning was a major consideration for system selection, and FCS scheduling sometimes took days. Compute speed remained a major consideration until a few years ago. The speed factor has essentially been eliminated except for very large and complex applications. The time to compute a typical application today is only a few minutes and diminishing. The speed and power of computers have been on an exponential growth curve and will remain on that curve. Speed does not need to be a consideration in the future.

Some major factors that constrain the success of FCS implementations vary with the application. Personnel, tracking, and updating are conditions that your company should consider before moving ahead to implement a modern scheduling system.

Personnel

Your personnel can be a major influence in determining the success or failure of an installation. All vendors have had implementations fail in one company when the same software was successful at installations in other companies with very similar conditions. Lack of proper training and acceptance by personnel can defeat good intentions. A small expense for education as early as possible goes a long way to ensure success and reduce the time and cost of installation. The early education and training allow time for personnel to discuss and accept the new scheduling paradigm.

Axiom #1—No Matter How Good a Software Package Is, If the Users Don't Have Ownership of the System, It Will Fail; Conversely, No Matter How Poor a Software Package Is, If the Users Have Ownership of the System, It Will Succeed.
Axiom # 2—Education Is a Critical Cost Element of Any Systems Implementation. If You Don't Pay for It before You Implement, You'll Pay for It Later On as You Clean Up the Mess!

Once your company decides to proceed with an installation, the training should include a definitive plan by management that fits with the strategy of the company, and this strategy must be communicated to all company personnel. As previously discussed, to be successful the FCS model must mirror the company strategy.

Tracking and Updating

Tracking and updating are important factors that will have a major impact on the level of success. The inability to absolutely predict every condition in the future implies that, at the time of rescheduling, the actual shop floor conditions will require coordination with the FCS conditions in the computer model.

Many options are available from manual updating to automated real-time tracking and updating. Reduced equipment cost will favor the manual end of the spectrum and accuracy and speed of rescheduling will favor the automated end. However, this is not assured at the outset. The task of coordinating the FCS system into a sophisticated tracking system can be arduous. Regardless of the tracking technique selected, the FCS model must be updated regularly to ensure a true representation of conditions on the shop floor prior to each rescheduling cycle.

The procedure for the development of a scheduling system is evolutionary. Designers of systems begin by implementing all conceivable functionality. As time passes and new client applications are presented, the designer is faced with adding functionality that was not perceived at the beginning of the design. The new supporting functionality often conflicts with one or more functions that exist in the current release. Each of these additional functions must be implemented and then rigorously tested until all conflicts are eliminated. This is a never-ending problem as functionality is added. This process, while disturbing for the short term, is necessary for progress and does not sabotage the long-term functionality.

Summary

We predict that FCS software will have a surge of activity as the Y2K problems pass. Improvement in scheduling is one area in manufacturing software that most users support. Now that the MRP/MRP II/ERP companies have finally acknowledged the need for modern scheduling and are either partnering or purchasing FCS companies, the industry is finally gaining acceptance and users will more actively pursue modern scheduling solutions.

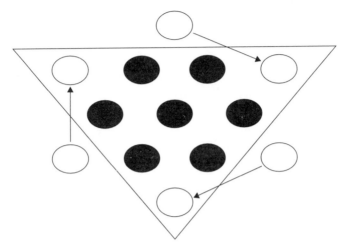

Figure 4.14   Ten Bowling Pins—Solution.

And what about the bowling pins? Figure 4.14 will help you turn your management structure upside down.

If You Fail to Plan (and Schedule), **You Plan to Fail.**

Part II

SCHEDULING METHODS

Chapter 5

Finite Capacity Scheduling

Capacity cost management is a journey, not a destination.
—C.J. McNair and Richard Vangermeersch,
Total Capacity Management

In a recent issue of *Meat and Poultry* magazine, editors quoted from *Feathers*, the publication of the California Poultry Industry Federation. They reported the U.S. Federal Aviation Administration (FAA) has a unique device for testing the strength of windshields on airplanes. The device is an air cannon that launches a dead chicken at a plane's windshield at the speed the plane flies. If the windshield doesn't crack from the impact, it'll survive a real collision with a bird in flight at similar speeds. The British Rail decided to use this method to test the windshields of their new, high-speed locomotives. They borrowed the FAA's chicken launcher, loaded a chicken, and fired. The high-speed chicken shattered the train's windshield, went through the engineer's chair, broke the instrument panel, and embedded itself in the back wall of the engine cab. The stunned engineers asked the FAA to review their test to see if everything was done correctly. The FAA validated the test thoroughly and came back with one recommendation: "Try thawing the chicken next time!" The moral of the story:

No system is better than its application!

With sales over $5.6 billion, Cummins Engine Company is the world's largest producer of diesel engines over 200 horsepower. Its Jamestown, New York, engine plant is one of 40 major plants and is a one-million-square-foot facility. It was experiencing all the pressures of a make-to-order environment:

Reduce lot sizes.

Reduce cycle times.

Deliver on time.

Increase productivity.

Using existing scheduling environments it suffered the frustrations of:

Difficulty in modeling all constraints.

Settling for "good enough" because of scheduling difficulties.

Difficulty handling scheduling changes.

Scheduling becoming, for the most part, a manual process.

After a four-month installation of an FCS environment it is now able to:

Generate 700 schedule simulations in less than a half hour.

Utilize rescheduling flexibility.

Optimize schedules.

Make real-time schedule adjustments.

The results of this implementation include:

There was a 90 percent reduction in cycle time.

Continuous improvement processes were implemented.

Inventory turns nearly doubled.

Schedule stability was greatly improved.

Of the many scheduling systems implemented in a broad range of manufacturing industries over the past 15 years, Bill cannot remember a single installation with simple and definitive solutions. The nature of manufacturing scheduling is inherently complex and the variables are in a continuous state of transition. Poorly managed production schedules can easily reach a state of chaos.

Manufacturers typically build to order, build to stock, or some combination of both. The current trend is build to order with high demand on short cycle times. Within this broad definition of business patterns we encounter conditions that are

127

uncontrollable or unpredictable which contribute to schedule instability and uncertainty.

This unpredictability means that scheduling is not going to be an exact science. A major scheduling objective is to minimize the unpredictability and stabilize the schedule for as long a time period as possible. Company scheduling decisions tend to be either strategic (long-term) to maintain continuity or tactical (intermediate-term), intended to meet all promised due dates in a dynamic environment. It is obvious that all companies want to maintain continuity and also meet promised due dates; however, these two conditions are in conflict, particularly when delivery dates are committed without adequate scheduling proficiency.

The next step should be to determine which scheduling method best fits your application. There is no absolute answer; however, if there is any bias for determining which method is the best fit, it is most likely dependent on a company's objectives and policies. Does the company desire to function on long-term scheduling stability or to ensure meeting due dates at all cost to satisfy clients? The following is the history of how we came to view the two management styles resulting in a correlation of the two operational philosophies.

As we implemented FCS systems to supplement MRP, we noticed that most companies were spending an excessive amount of time and money in the process of expediting jobs. Due dates would be promised to clients based on MRP logic. In spite of the fact that the due dates were based on long lead times, many jobs risked being late as the due date approached.

The inability to predict finish dates was the source of the problem that led to inaccurate promise dates. The response was to expedite a job as its due date approached, then expedite the next job, and so on, literally creating a perpetual process of expediting. This pattern seemed to be the universal solution—it surfaced in company after company, particularly when product demand was high.

Over time we noticed that management decisions in companies with high expediting were made predominantly to satisfy customer demands. This often meant promising unrealistic delivery dates. We observed that if delivery dates could be accurately predicted and promise dates were based on reality as calculated by the FCS system, then expediting would be eliminated, or, at minimum, dramatically reduced.

Unfortunately, at a number of companies this did not happen when the FCS system was implemented. Even though the FCS system produced reliable dates, the schedule was not followed. Sales would make promises to get orders and then revise promise dates without referring to the FCS schedule. The old habits of satisfying customer demands at the expense of the schedule did not go away. This led to numerous companies stopping their use of the FCS system and returning to traditional practices. Regardless of what system is used, unrealistic promises that cause demand to exceed capacity result in either late delivery for some customers or excessive expenses to create extra capacity to meet promises, and of course expediting. Management must decide when it is expedient to turn down orders.

Because of these observations, we created the concept of two scheduling management styles:

➢ Capacity management.

➢ Job management.

The objective of capacity management is to meet all constraints with emphasis on maximizing resource utilization. This approach presupposes an efficient operation and a management strategy that is willing to turn down a customer order to maintain production efficiency and high customer on-time delivery performance.

The objective of job management is to meet all constraints with emphasis on meeting customer demands. This approach presupposes maintaining customer satisfaction at the expense of production efficiency. A tactical management style implies excess capacity through the use of overtime or some other means. Capacity expansion is a standard practice used to meet delivery dates.

It is unlikely that any company will rigidly fit into either end of the management spectrum. It is important to acknowledge that the two styles are conflicting in their objective and that selecting a scheduling system will depend on a company's strategic objectives.

Neither style is promoted as the preferred management style. Management objectives vary by company and the scheduling system must be able to adapt to management objectives. Having said that, any of the three FCS methods discussed in the previous chapters will deliver feasible schedules at either end of this management spectrum. This is one reason it is not possible to make absolute statements or to draw a universal conclusion. As stated previously, many feasible solutions are possible from any FCS system. The intent is to select a scheduling system that repeatedly produces the best results based on company objectives and is most adaptable to the company's operating procedures. Realistic promise dates can be accomplished by either approach if promise dates to the client conform to dates calculated by FCS scheduling logic. Our observations are that the event-based methods correspond best to companies that prefer operating in a strategic, long-term mode, and the job-based method is more adaptable to companies that desire to function in a tactical, short-term mode.

Figure 5.1 is a graph for evaluating the penalty for expediting. The graph shows how productivity efficiency declines when there is a deviation from the theoretical optimal (minimum) cost for processing jobs. A job that takes longer for processing than the ideal condition suffers a slight increase from the optimum cost, while a job that is expedited results in a significant increase in cost. Deviation in either direction is undesirable; however, this figure clearly shows why expediting should be avoided whenever possible. Small improvements in job cycle time cause a significant increase in actual cost as compared to the optimum minimum cost. It is expensive to promise due dates that force jobs into the expedite mode.

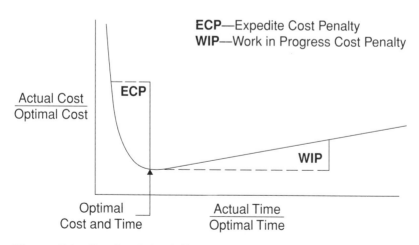

Figure 5.1 Productivity Efficiency.

SELECTING A METHOD

No specific method is being promoted or recommended; however, there are unique characteristics about each method that tend to make each one a better fit for specific management objectives. The scheduling method your company selects should be based on the company's objectives and operating procedures.

The sequence of the selection process should be:

1. Determine the company management style.

2. Define operating procedures and policies.

3. Define strategic, tactical, and operational parameters to be followed within the defined operating procedures and policies.

Selecting the management style implies establishing the company's fundamental principles. The company's management style may seem to be self-evident, but stating it as a policy establishes it as a direction for all employees.

Defining strategic operating procedures and policies takes us a step closer to a refined plan. This involves management committing to strategic positions that define company policies and procedures. Defining strategic and tactical parameters creates the functional structure that will be used to model the FCS system. Strategic parameters tend to remain constant in the FCS model, and tactical parameters are subject to change at any time for any number of reasons. Machine failure is an example that would effect a tactical change in the model.

Event-based systems tend to be more strategic because they schedule by moving forward in time and scheduling all resources at the task level on a minute-by-minute basis. At each moment, for every resource, the EBM makes decisions based on the strategic objective established by the company and avoids wasted capacity when demand exists.

Job-based systems schedule jobs based on the job priority. Since the JBM schedules all tasks in each job out in time based on job priority, it is easier to get a visual picture of what might happen when manual adjustments are made.

Regardless of the method selected, accurately modeling the FCS system to conform to the company strategy is an important and necessary step. Strategy in the traditional sense includes the establishment of operational procedures and policies that are followed by company personnel. Strategy as applied to MRP/ERP systems tends to be isolated from the tactical and operational functions. Once long-term strategic decisions are implemented, tactical and operational planning follows and is repeated on a cyclical basis, retaining a focus on the strategic plan.

Strategy as applied to FCS systems requires that strategic, tactical, and operational policies be implemented in the model such that conditions that occur at all three levels are considered in each scheduling cycle. The strategic conditions remain constant for long time periods, and the tactical conditions are adjusted randomly as required prior to each scheduling cycle. Operational conditions are less definitive, and changes are typically made on the shop floor as they occur. Operational changes are relatively small deviations from the schedule, and the deviations generally do not trigger updating and rescheduling.

No system will produce a flawless schedule. Therefore, tracking of actual shop floor conditions is required to allow for updating to coordinate shop floor conditions to the FCS system prior to scheduling the next cycle. A standard scheduling cycle time (day/week/month) is a predetermined time frame. When a major unpredictable condition occurs within the scheduling cycle, it will be necessary to update actual conditions prior to the end of the cycle. The unpredictable event triggers a tactical adjustment and usually triggers a need to reschedule prior to the end of the standard scheduling cycle. A workstation failure in a bottleneck work center that requires several days of downtime for maintenance would be an example of an unpredictable tactical condition requiring premature updating and rescheduling. A failure in a noncritical workstation that has buffer capacity would not cause rescheduling prior to the end of the cycle.

Since each method considers and manages all constraints and generates feasible schedules, the only absolute way to determine which method and ultimately which vendor offers the best solution for your application is to create a set of data that models your application and allows thorough testing and comparison of the vendors. The development of a data set to test vendors has become known as a scripted demo.

The power of FCS is based on its ability to:

1. Model the company's strategy.

2. Manage all constraints imposed on the system.

3. Make random adjustments to tactical conditions.

4. Function without rescheduling when small shop deviations occur.

5. Produce accurate schedules that allow for predictable delivery dates.

134

To benefit from FCS, the company must ensure:

1. That the schedule is followed.

2. That the strategic and tactical adjustments are made within the FCS system.

3. That the tracking system produces accurate data for updating work status.

We again refer to Table 4.1—Capacity Cost Management Phases as defined by C.J. McNair and Richard Vangermeersch in their book *Total Capacity Management. Total Capacity Management* describes numerous accounting methods for calculating capacity that have been used for the past hundred years. It discusses the controversy that has existed over time about measuring capacity. The ability of the FCS system to accurately define capacity will reduce and ultimately eliminate the controversy.

A recent thread from www.mfg-info@list.msu.edu divulged just how much controversy is currently prevalent. The comments on the list were abundant, with diverse opinions expressed. Little agreement was evident from the members of the list on how to measure and manage capacity.

The McNair/Vangermeersch book's dialogue on capacity management measurement is from an accounting perspective. Their use of the three time periods of strategic (long-term), tactical (intermediate-term), and operational (short-term) phases for accounting corresponds to what we advocate as the best approach for modeling FCS applications. Their book evaluates 12 methods of measuring capacity and states that there is no one model that suits every need. We maintain that implementing FCS will assist in accurately and dynamically maintaining the company database and will, as a result, also ensure more accurate data to assist in capacity measurement for accounting purposes regardless of the model your company selects.

What we are suggesting will not eliminate the ongoing argument of how to manage the accounting functions related to capacity. Nor does it show us how to allocate idle capacity and other debatable accounting issues. It does, however, offer a method that ensures accurate measuring of resource utilization by product, down to individual machines. This is a prerequisite for determining product costing.

Determining accurate resource utilization with FCS is an inherent function since the FCS system never exceeds the capacity available or any other constraint included in the model. Work center reports and graphics clearly show resources in use over time. In contrast, MRP work center Capacity Requirements Planning (CRP) reports show periods that exceed available capacity anytime a bottleneck is encountered, even a short-term bottleneck.

DATA ACCURACY

Data consistency is a prerequisite for accurate scheduling. The tracking system must deliver accurate data to the scheduling system. Some tracking applications produce undesirable results and it is a common practice to use the FCS system to test consistency of the imported tracking data. The FCS consistency testing does not absolutely ensure that all bad data is eliminated; it does, however, ensure that no unfeasible data gets by. Using FCS to monitor for consistency is not enough. Once an error is detected, it must be resolved before scheduling the next production cycle. Most companies find that the tracking methods traditionally used result in enough defective data that it is necessary to modify tracking practices when FCS is implemented.

The FCS systems are capable of performing consistency checks because they never violate any constraint that has been modeled. In contrast, MRP systems are not equipped to handle all constraints, which prohibits the ability to check for consistency.

MANUFACTURING TIME PHASES

The three time phases as defined by McNair and Vanger-meersch and shown in Table 4.1 are strategic (long-term), tactical (intermediate-term), and operational (short-term). The level of management responsible for monitoring and maintaining the function is an additional indication of whether the time phase is strategic, tactical, or operational.

The FCS systems offer management the ability to critically analyze and evaluate the effect of strategic and tactical adjustments in a simulated what-if mode of operation. If the results of examining a parameter prove desirable, the new parameter can be implemented as permanent.

The FCS systems universally allow for modeling the different management phases. How this is accomplished is a function of each vendor's FCS system. Regardless of the system selected, a company must become familiar with how to model the system of choice. The good news about FCS systems is that they place much of the power into the hands of the user. The user therefore must learn to control this power. Learning FCS modeling skills is a process that allows for continual production improvement.

Most companies view their operations as unique. However, we see less uniqueness in scheduling than is perceived by most. Scheduling is the art of coordinating previous and following operations without violating constraints. A task is a task regardless of whether its duration is one minute, one day, or one month, or whether it is managing a steel mill, a computer factory, airline maintenance schedules, or, as in one example in Brisbane, Australia, a hospital. Scheduling involves coordinating tasks within jobs through work centers, and the same disciplines apply regardless of the product or cycle times. Where companies are truly unique is in the operational policies of each individual company. The modeling power to manage this uniqueness is offered by FCS systems. It is the responsibility of the client to become competent in applying the software.

Even the most ardent companies that identify themselves as strategic will at times deviate from their strategy and make tactical moves that are not considered to be in their charter. FCS systems make it possible to manage the tactical adjustments with minimum impact on strategic goals.

Tactical decisions are by definition divergences from standard or scheduled operation. Tactical moves can be very positive for realigning resources to improve short-term throughput, then reverting to strategic positions. These changes can be the result of a shift in demand, resource downtime, or any number of unpredictable conditions.

Summary

Defining objectives is the first task in selecting an FCS system; next is analyzing which one of the many FCS alternatives will be the best fit for those objectives. Each methodology has its advantages, but ultimately the best procedure is to narrow your selection down to a few systems that seem to be a good fit, then script a test of your live data and run it against each of these systems. Only with this test will you be able to ultimately define which system will do the best job in your environment.

> The measure of success is not whether you have a tough problem to deal with, but whether it's the same problem you had last year.
>
> —JOHN FOSTER DULLES

Chapter 6

What the Future Holds

Technology is the continuation of evolution by other means, and is itself an evolutionary process. . . . The evolutionary process of technology seeks to improve capabilities in an exponential fashion. Innovators seek to improve things by multiples. Innovation is multiplicative, not additive. Technology, like any other evolutionary process, builds on itself. This aspect will continue to accelerate when the technology itself takes full control of its own progression.
—RAY KURZWEIL, *The Age of Spiritual Machines*
(New York: Viking, 1999)

Bill Kirchmier recalls a graphic from when he attended Michigan State University in the middle 1950s. He has re-drawn it as Figure 6.1 (original source unknown).

This graph has repeatedly proven to be on the mark. The average citizens do not perceive progress; they accept it when it is delivered. Engineers and scientists view progress as a linear function. But history shows that innovations actually take place at an exponential rate, far exceeding expectations. Consider the following examples of exponential advancements since the beginning of the twentieth century. Transportation has gone from very slow speeds to spaceship velocities with several major paradigm shifts. Horses were replaced by cars and trains, albeit not a lot faster when the

141

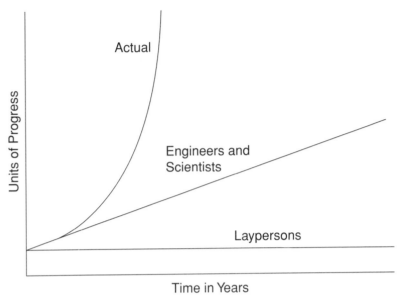

Figure 6.1 Perceptions of Innovation.

shift began (but speeds continued to increase, and even to-day train speeds are continuing to rise). The next shift was to air travel using internal combustion engines, then to jet engines, then to space travel with rockets. A similar pattern in communications and computers can be illustrated. Examples of exponential growth in information and communication technology are currently taking place, and information technology is the driving force behind the continuously improving economy in the United States. It is at the base of all of today's commercial activity.

Note the sequence of events that is repeated in the information technology process. The first action is the creation of new or better hardware systems. This increased capacity in hardware fosters the development of more powerful software. This in turn improves the operating efficiency for companies that buy and use the hardware and software, fueling a renewed demand for faster computers, then again improved software, which results in a new cycle.

The first businesses to benefit from modern computer processing were financial, insurance, and other sectors that required repetitive calculations that were generally quite simple. One example is the management of materials, which is the repetitive process of ordering and maintaining inventory levels. The evolution of MRP-MRP II-ERP software over the past 30 years is a case in point. This family of software is and has been the default solution for manufacturing companies. The transition from MRP to ERP has been fairly smooth with each step in the process being a natural progression of adding capacity in the form of additional applications and/or improving capability within the existing modules. This is a normal progression. Also normal is that technology reaches a point that requires a shift in the process in order for any significant progress to continue—that is, for a new paradigm shift to take place.

Finite scheduling is the current paradigm shift for manufacturing software. The shift is not yet self-evident. Resistance has been high. However, utilization of FCS software has reached a critical mass and is now gaining devoted users. As developers and users acquire more experience, the next natural progression will take place. The MRP and ERP system designs will give way to a more effective way of managing materials and capacity resources. This generation of manufacturing software will completely eliminate the application of infinite capacity systems, which will impact traditional vendors. The type of software companies that win this new battle for the next generation of software is still undetermined. Several possibilities are shaping up to be contenders.

The first and most obvious prospects for FCS are the traditional MRP/ERP vendors. Although ERP has lost much of its appeal, it retains several advantages. They exist firmly with a large base of clients that would like to maintain continuity and minimize the effort of implementing new software. Changing software is always expensive and impacts business while the change is underway.

The Internet is causing business models to change. This creates yet another barrier for the more traditional systems that are typically managed by only a few personnel in the organization. Systems were maintained on a limited-access basis by all personnel in the company who need to access the database. Changing traditional software to accommodate the value of the Internet is time-consuming and expensive.

Although the MRP/ERP group has been resisting the change for at least 10 years, many are now finally moving to include finite scheduling. The question becomes whether they are too late to recover. We pointed out earlier that the past two years has seen a surge of action by MRP/ERP vendors to acquire or partner with FCS vendors. Their delay in taking action has created an opportunity for the innovators to gain entrance and a possible advantage.

In addition, the MRP/ERP group is saddled with disadvantages. Converting to a concept that makes use of FCS will require elimination of the infinite capacity assumptions. It will require the redesign and the elimination of many lines of code that supports infinite capacity software. The establishment that waits too long to convert is always at risk of losing control.

At least two groups can be defined as threatening to become the preferred suppliers. They are the independent FCS vendors and the Advanced Planning and Scheduling (APS)

vendors. Confusion can arise since there is no pure definition of what APS really is. One can argue that APS software
is based on a finite scheduler with additional software applications for the other business functions. Some APS vendors
currently offer material modules, while others claim to be
content to interface with existing vendors that offer material
systems. Most likely FCS vendors joining forces with independent best-of-breed material systems vendors and vendors of other system applications (financial, forecasting,
distribution, maintenance, etc.) will be an influence in
changing the market.

Then there is the Supply Chain Management (SCM) con-
tingent, whose strong suit is combining vendors' and customers' information with the manufacturers' data. Prospects
evaluating and selecting software for the future truly have a
mix of potential directions. The lines are very unclear.

A major factor of this transition is the drive from materials management to capacity management. The recent effort
by manufacturers to reduce inventory levels has been so successful that the emphasis has now shifted to reducing cycle
times. This benefit must come from the capacity side of the
equation. Reducing cycle time is one of the principal attributes of FCS. The transition in a system focus to cycle time reduction has become very apparent.

There is little agreement on the best approach. Each vendor will argue for a chosen point of view as being best.
Prospects evaluating systems must ultimately make their decisions based on conflicting and confusing information.
Prospects also must evaluate the level of expertise required
to implement a system. There is a considerable contrast in the
degree of difficulty of implementing the various scheduling
methods and even differences in the way you can implement
vendors that apply the same method.

> Once You've Chosen the Road,
> You've Chosen the Destination.

THE ART OF EVALUATING FCS SCHEDULING SYSTEMS

We have discussed in detail the methods used by scheduling vendors to develop FCS systems and stated that each of the FCS systems is capable of delivering numerous feasible schedules. The selection process is additionally complicated when numerous systems are to be evaluated, each of which offers a number of feasible schedules. Prospects must make decisions on how to evaluate scheduling systems based on their unique applications. The use of a scripted demo offers the best approach and eliminates internal controversy. With the scripted demo, a company needs to create a strategy for the scripted demo evaluation.

The term *scripted demo* has evolved to describe the process of compiling a set of data to be used to evaluate vendor software. This approach determines which vendors have the mix of features and functions best suited to schedule a specific application. It is a process of elimination. You are left with the vendors that schedule your application most effectively. Then you would use traditional evaluation methods to select the final vendor.

The primary purpose of the scripted demo is to ensure that each vendor receives identical data. This way we can compare vendors on a level playing field. Once the data is compiled and tested for accuracy, it can be sent to vendors in machine-readable format.

The following is a list of fundamental attributes that should be evaluated when selecting finite scheduling software.

146

1. Scheduling competence.

2. Interfacing.

3. Modeling.

4. Tracking and updating.

5. Graphical user interface (GUI).

6. What-if options.

7. Reports and graphics.

8. Drag and drop.

Each function is important. However, scheduling capability is the preeminent reason for purchasing a scheduling system and it is often the least-evaluated aspect of the software. Too often, prospects concentrate on system selection based on the modeling function, graphical user interface (GUI), or other functions without considering scheduling competence.

As previously discussed, infinite capacity scheduling software functioned as a planning system and did not perform detailed scheduling. Infinite scheduling never demanded the serious evaluation that should be used for selecting finite scheduling software.

It is common for prospects to assume that MRP files can be used to create the data for a scripted demo. However, numerous calculations are performed by FCS systems that surpass MRP functionality and require more data fields. The following is a list of functions requiring data that is not available in MRP/ERP systems or at least not available in sufficient detail. Numerous examples could be added to the list.

➤ Overlapping tasks.

➤ Multiple resource constraints.

➤ Splitting tasks for a single operation.

➤ Setup minimization.

➤ Preferred workstations.

➤ Alternate work centers.

➤ Variable shift patterns by work center.

➤ Variable capacity over time.

Data for the scripted demo can be compiled manually. However, this approach is not likely to result in an indisputable evaluation. The probability is high that vendors will interpret manually compiled data differently and minimize the validity of the evaluation. Evaluation results will not be comparable if interpretation of the input data is left to the vendor. The best solution to ensure both data consistency and constraint consistency is to use a finite scheduling engine to create and test the data. Using a scheduling engine to model and schedule the application also establishes a benchmark for comparison with the competing vendor results.

Since companies looking for scheduling systems are not likely to have access to a finite scheduling engine, they may need consulting assistance or to work with a vendor in establishing the benchmark. Care must be taken to eliminate the possibility of biased data when using a vendor system.

The minimum data files necessary for a comprehensive scripted demo are:

1. Work center.

2. Routings.

3. Jobs (work orders).

4. Calendar by work center.

5. Bill of materials (BOM) if assembly relations exist.

Chapter 4 contains minimal examples of the data that is required for a scripted demo. No standard can be established due to the vast differences in applications.

The purpose of scheduling is for resolving conflicts and meeting objectives. For best results, the scripted demo should investigate all the possible conflicts that exist in your application. A procedure for structuring the demo to measure vendor performance is to compare vendor results based on the time it takes to process a definitive set of work orders (demand) through a definitive set of resources (capacity). A vendor's success will be based on its system's ability to effectively manage all constraints while minimizing overall cycle time. This approach leaves each vendor free to use any scheduling routines, features, and functions in its software arsenal.

Each vendor is responsible for reducing the many feasible solutions to the best solution for the application being modeled. It is therefore necessary for the vendor to comprehend the conditions that are being measured and then confirm them against the constraints. Vendors are often inclined to think they know what is best for the client and deviate from the conditions established for the application. Deviation from the objective usually eliminates the vendor from the competition.

The demo must include enough work orders (demand) to overload capacity and create queuing. Any FCS system will handle underloaded workloads. Your objective must be to isolate capable systems by creating complex demands and conflicts normally associated with your application.

An example of a common scheduling conflict could be attempting to minimize setup while meeting all promised finish dates. Trade-offs will be necessary. If your company is interested in meeting due dates, you can be assured that reducing setup is likely to impact some promise dates. Compromises must be built into the model based on a company strategy to resolve these conflicts.

Within this context you can also compare vendors on any other conditions that are important to your company strategy. This is accomplished by structuring the model to include the testing of all conditions that are important to your application. The scripted demo approach results in an unbiased comparison of top contenders and quickly eliminates vendors with less scheduling capability for your specific application. Vendor success will vary by application.

Some vendors that promote GUI features or drag and drop capability will resist the scripted demo approach. However, the resistance will most likely be due to an acknowledged weakness in scheduling ability.

MANAGEMENT STYLES

We have observed two management styles that are predominant for managing shop floor production and have designated them as job management and capacity management. Neither style is being promoted. Both represent conventional company strategies. The reference is to indicate that selecting a vendor will involve matching the method that best fits your company strategy. Any of the methods can be used for either management style, but not with the same results. Also, multiple vendors applying the same method will yield different results, which is a strong reason to create a comprehensive set of evaluation data.

The objective of job management is to satisfy customer demands. This style is biased toward making dynamic tactical adjustments as required to meet customer demand. This approach presupposes excess capacity and customer satisfaction at the expense of production efficiency, and may require excessive expediting. Job-based FCS scheduling methods most closely fit the job management style. The job-based method schedules at the job level and blocks out resources downstream to ensure resources are available for higher-priority jobs.

The emphasis of capacity management is on maximizing resource utilization and minimizing cycle time of each job and the overall cycle time of all jobs. The event-based scheduling method most closely fits the capacity management style. The event-based method schedules at the task level and results in higher resource utilization. It is a valuable tool for companies that prefer to maximize throughput and minimize tactical decisions as much as possible. This approach presupposes an efficient utilization of resources. Management is more willing to turn down an order to maintain production efficiency and thereby gain longer-term overall predictability. Companies that use the capacity management style are less inclined to make tactical adjustments, but the option for adjustment is always available.

Scheduling strategy is implemented by judicious decisions during development of the FCS scheduling model, giving the user unlimited control over model development with either scheduling method. In summary, the purpose of a scripted demo is to create a set of structured data that represents all constraints in the application and leaves no room for vendor interpretation. This ensures that all vendors use identical input. The vendor is free to apply any scheduling features and functionality available to accomplish meeting the prospect-defined scheduling objectives.

EXAMPLES

This book has listed a number of success stories describing the implementation of FCS systems in plants. Here is an example of a scheduler developed independently in a university environment. This system, called Schedule Based Manufacturing (SBM), has created a great deal of excitement in Southeast Asia because of its ability to outperform traditional MRP environments. Without endorsing this product in any way, we include this story as an example of a system designed to advance scheduling. We do not consider this to be an FCS system as defined in the book; however, it supports the philosophy of the book—that MRP technology has become dated and that scheduling needs to be addressed by any company that continues to depend on MRP planning concepts. See Appendix 6.1 for the detailed story.

SUMMARY

This chapter has discussed the shift that is taking place in manufacturing software and defines an approach for selecting effective FCS scheduling software. Having selected the software that best fits our environment, we can now move forward with its implementation.

Thee lift me and I'll lift thee, and we'll ascend together.

—Quaker proverb

SBM—Schedule Based Manufacturing: The Advantages of an Integrated Solution of Materials and Resources for Manufacturers

Dr. J. R. Barker

The paper shows why the existing MRP II, because of "horizontal" and "vertical" separation, cannot satisfactorily solve the problem of ensuring that resources and materials are available on the shop floor when needed at each production stage. To achieve high productivity, materials and resources *must* be available simultaneously; there are penalties for either late or early availability. This is a classical, practical

This Appendix is excerpted from a 21-page article. The author is an Associate Professor and Associate Dean of the School of Information Technology, Bond University, Queensland, 4229, Australia. *Tel.* 61 7 5595-3344, *fax* 61 7 5595-3320, *e-mail* jeff_barker@bond.edu.au.

manufacturing problem that may severely limit a factory's productivity.

The paper then defines an enhanced MRP II philosophy, called SBM (Schedule Based Manufacturing), which encompasses the existing MRP II, JIT, and OPT philosophies. The results are given of implementing SBM in two factories.

INTRODUCTION

Manufacturers have been plagued by the problem of ensuring that resources (machines, labor, tools, jigs, transport, storage, etc.) and materials (raw or manufactured) are available on the shop floor when needed at each production stage. Simultaneously, costs are to be kept at a minimum to ensure profitability and customer due-dates are to be met to ensure customer satisfaction. Costs are minimized by ensuring that raw material, work in progress material, and resources (especially labor) are maintained at the lowest possible levels with no excess.

Two main manufacturing philosophies have been used to date, MRP II (Manufacturing Resource Planning) and JIT (Just In Time) with varying degrees of success. OPT, a philosophy and a computer application package, has also been used, again with varying success levels.

The suitability of JIT may be summarized as follows:

➢ Suitable for repetitive "make-to-order" manufacturers.

➢ Maybe good for job shops in certain circumstances.

➢ Need small set-up times.

➤ Need co-operative suppliers—JIT deliveries.

➤ Often creates problems for suppliers.

➤ Not suitable for many manufacturers.

➤ Bit "selfish"—not all links (manufacturers) in a manufacturing chain can use it.

This paper introduces an enhanced MRP II philosophy for manufacturers, called SBM, and will concentrate on its comparison with MRP II as this is still by far the most frequently used manufacturing philosophy in Asia.

CORPORATE CONFLICTS

The corporate objective of most manufacturers is to make a profit and this can be achieved in various ways, some of which are conflicting and therefore require a certain amount of balancing. The best known of these is the conflict between improving customer service and lowering costs. Good customer service requires factors such as timely delivery, correct quantity, correct quality, manufacturing flexibility, short runs, etc. Lower costs, on the other hand, are usually achieved with fewer set-ups, longer runs, maximization of machine utilization, etc.

Other conflicts can arise within an organization in trying to achieve the corporate objective. The *finance* department targets greater efficiencies and bigger margins. *Manufacturing* strives to be more effective and to minimize waste. *Logistics* want to minimize stock (raw, WIP, and finished goods) whilst the *sales* department wants to maximize sales by having required quantities of stock being available (make to stock or make to order) when customers want it.

Perhaps the most crucial component in the manufacturing planning process is the determination and synchronization of the correct amount of materials and resources on the shop floor to maximize customer service and minimize costs. Three manufacturing philosophies (MRP II, JIT, and OPT) have been used to help manufacturers in this task. *JIT* (Just In Time) can be used where the manufacturing lead time is less than the required delivery time and no forecasting is needed. *OPT* (Optimized Production Technology) is both a philosophy and a package. *MRP II* (Manufacturing Resource Planning) is currently the most widely used philosophy.

Materials Requirements and Resources Planning

It has been shown many times in the literature that MRP II (Manufacturing Resource Planning) in its current form is, at best, an approximating philosophy for manufacturing (see the above references). The philosophy grew out of the reasonable success of MRP (Materials Requirements Planning). The term *reasonable success* is used because MRP was superior to the then current alternatives (EOQ, reorder points, etc.) which ordered for the future based on what happened in the past. MRP ordered for the future based on forecast and/or actual future requirements. These future requirements were "fed" to the MRP via an MPS (Master Production Schedule). Manufacturers could at least plan ahead, albeit very roughly.

Rough cut capacity planning was then introduced to try to determine if enough capacity was available to "service" the generated MRP. If enough capacity was not available, the MPS would be massaged, another MRP generated, and capacity again tested. This cycle would continue until an MRP was generated which did not *appear* to overload capacity. This procedure was termed MRP II. It was an improvement over what had been used previously and many manufacturers implemented it, with varying levels of success, using commercially available software packages. A *simplified* schematic of the existing MRP II philosophy is given in Figure 6.2.

Problems with the current MRP II and its implementa-

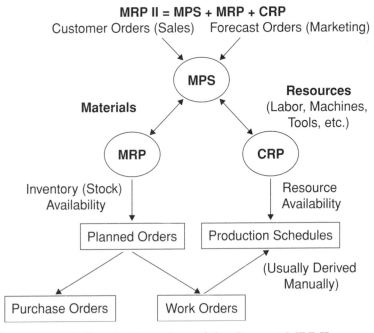

Figure 6.2 A Simple Overview of the Current MRP II Philosophy.

tion have been well documented (again, see the above references). Some of these have been summarized as follows:

> ➤ Lack of management commitment.
> ➤ Routings and bills may be separate.
> ➤ Lack of education.
> ➤ "Demotivating" process.
> ➤ Lot size; same for transfer as for process.
> ➤ Long implementation time.
> ➤ Lead times are static in MRP II but not in reality (schedule related).
> ➤ Lead times usually have to be determined and then entered (schedule related).
> ➤ Forward scheduling vs. backward scheduling (schedule related).
> ➤ Unrealistic MPSs do not consider actual job sequencing (schedule related).
> ➤ Lack of accurate data (schedule related).
> ➤ Requires a lot of human and computer resources (schedule related).
> ➤ Continual manual time-consuming adjustment is necessary (schedule related).

As Browne[1] mentions, MRP II "sought sophistication but found complexity instead." The lead times used were static but the manufacturing processes were dynamic.

I propose that the inherent problems with the existing

---

[1]Browne, J., Harhen, J., and J. Shivnan, *Production Management Systems: A CIM Perspective*, Reading, MA: Addison-Wesley Publishing Company, Inc., 1988.

MRP II are what I term the vertical and horizontal separations. MRP II separates planned production (MPS) from actual production (actual shop floor schedule). I have termed this the vertical separation. It also separates materials from resources when determining material requirements (MRP) and resource requirements (CRP or Capacity Resource Planning). I have termed this the horizontal separation. This is illustrated, in a simplified manner, in Figure 6.3.

Many of the problems listed above relate to horizontal or vertical separation. Other problems with MRP II include:

> Sequences dependencies are not considered (schedule related).

> Shop floor loadings are not considered in MRP (schedule related).

> Difficulty with multiple machines per work center: different capacities, speeds, and/or capabilities (schedule related).

> Dynamic relationships between resources and materials are not considered (schedule related).

> Tries to balance capacity rather than flow (schedule related).

> Interjob dependencies are not considered (schedule related).

Real-Time Interactive Scheduling

In the 1980s an Australian software company introduced an interactive shop floor scheduler called OPS (Online Produc-

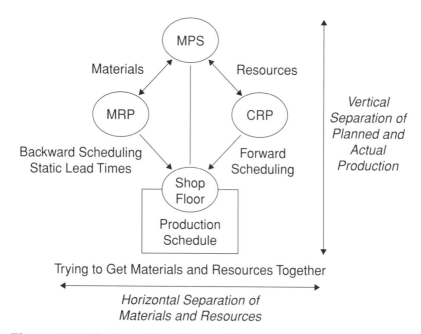

Figure 6.3   Horizontal and Vertical Separation of the Current MRP II Philosophy.

tion Scheduler), based on the work of and developed by Associate Professor G. McMahon and the author. OPS did not consider material requirements at all. It scheduled shop orders for actual capacity (resources) available. The resultant Gantt chart was displayed graphically on an x-window terminal. The production planning staff could then "edit" the schedule with a mouse to satisfy any "informal" constraints if such action was required. Schedules could be copied allowing "what-if" analysis. Resources could be added, modified, and/or deleted to analyze the effect of such alterations on the existing and known future workload (shop orders).

To quote Browne et al., "In our view, finite scheduling is appropriate at the PAC (production activity control) level. In particular, we believe that OPT type scheduling will find application in the scheduler building block of future PAC systems. However, we do not believe that the OPT approach, in terms of blindly following machine developed schedules, will find wide acceptance. Our concept is that one must have real-time scheduling or dispatching to allow supervisors and operators to control their environment in terms of their up-to-date knowledge of the manufacturing system."

Although OPS was being used before the above was published, that view expresses quite well the initial *raison d'etre* for OPS.

The first client who used OPS simply wanted to produce finished goods for customers on time. The client, a large discrete manufacturer, quoted a delivery time of 6 weeks (manufacturing time was 5.5 weeks average) but was almost always around 6 weeks late; i.e., actual delivery time was 12 weeks on average instead of the quoted 6 weeks. Manufacturing problems within the company included:

> ➤ Late jobs (almost all jobs).

> ➤ Plenty of WIP inventory.

> ➤ Crisis scheduling.

> ➤ No production schedule was available.

> ➤ Bad customer relations.

> ➤ Bad relations between manufacturing and sales (the deadly embrace).

After implementing OPS, not only were jobs produced on time, but raw materials, WIP, and finished goods inventory went down to previously unattainable levels, saving the manufacturer millions of dollars. Materials requirements and inventory were obviously a function of resources. Further, other benefits occurred including decreased manufacturing times (not predicted) and a reduction of "job expeditors" from eight to one. The manufacturer's own results on what happened due to the implementation of OPS are given at the end of this paper. These are summarized below:

➢ Suspicion initially.

➢ Jobs on time.

➢ No WIP inventory.

➢ Diminishing finished goods inventory.

➢ Availability of what-if analysis.

➢ Production manager went on holidays.

➢ Good customer relations.

➢ Good relations between manufacturing and sales departments.

➢ Huge $ savings.

Another manufacturer, in the clothing industry, cut down production planning time from *12 days per month to 30 minutes*. This enabled the company to review progress daily if required and to plan production twice weekly instead of once monthly. As a bonus, inventory also went down to previously unattainable levels. Both of these manufacturers were using MRP II packages before OPS was implemented.

The success of OPS has proven the worth of interactive real-time scheduling.

ACHIEVED IMPROVEMENTS DUE TO INTERACTIVE SCHEDULING

Quite a few schedulers are now appearing on the market reflecting the demand for such products and the amount of research and development going into such products. OPS has been implemented in a number of commercial manufacturing sites with most of these sites using the interactive x-window graphics version. The achieved improvements for those manufacturers using OPS included:

Better Schedules

The computerized schedules are typically superior (more factual) to the previous schedules because they are created from "actual" data rather than "approximate" data.

Speed of Schedule Generation

The actual production scheduling process was previously done manually or with "simple" computer aids and took either hours or days to complete. Most, if not all, of the required calculations were repetitious; i.e., they were performed many times for just one schedule. These calculations are done in minutes with OPS.

This not only helped for future schedules, it also helped when unexpected problems occurred. For example, if one or more machines broke down and required unplanned maintenance, a new schedule was required for certain orders to be completed on time. Without OPS, it took a long time to manually determine how these breakdowns (for example) affected the current production schedule and then generate a new one. With OPS it was done within minutes.

Multiple Schedules and What-Ifs

More than one schedule can be generated. If desired, many schedules can be created because of the speed of OPS. Only one schedule, of course, is the actual production schedule being used. Multiple schedules allow the production planners and others to carry out what-if analysis such as:

> ➤ What if capacity was increased by purchasing more machines?

> ➤ What would be the effect of moving some production forward or backward?

> ➤ What if labor changes were made?

> ➤ What if the quantities and/or due-dates for orders were changed?

> ➤ What would be the effect on other orders if an urgent (but profitable) as yet unscheduled order was scheduled?

> ➤ What if materials do not arrive on time?

Knowledge Sharing

Scheduling knowledge is encapsulated on the computer. This releases a lot of pressure from the production planning staff and enables the manufacturer to more easily share the scheduling knowledge between employees, when and if required. It also ensures that the manufacturer always has the scheduling knowledge and can improve and build on it if so desired.

Orders Are Manufactured When Required

Orders were planned to be manufactured before they are actually required. This meant that actual requirements, time wise, were hidden, production was bought forward, and completed orders were stored as finished goods for possibly much longer than necessary. OPS simply schedules the orders to be completed before or on the day that they are required. Time buckets are not necessary but can still be used, if desired, for report and review purposes.

Cut Down Physical Storage Requirements

It is now possible to plan raw material requirements more accurately and hence receive more timely supplies of certain materials. For some clients, this means that less storage capacity is required to store raw materials. Finished orders are also completed much closer to when they are needed thus requiring storage for much shorter lengths of time. This further cuts down physical storage requirements.

Schedule Editing

The schedule is graphically displayed on an x-window terminal for the production planner to assess and, if desired, modify. A schedule can be copied (many times if necessary) and modified to determine the effects of doing a particular change. Many changes can be made and tested with the option of simply recalling the original schedule (or any other schedule) if and when required. The "what-if" facility is dealt with below.

An x-window work station also has the benefit of displaying many windows simultaneously. More than one schedule can be on the screen as well as, say, the original order data.

Schedule Comparison

Production planners typically have not had the luxury previously of generating more than one schedule. OPS allows them to generate more than one and to do so in minutes. This creates the problem of how to compare two schedules to determine which is superior. Such a comparison can be done on the window terminal (graphically) by looking for and comparing certain critical jobs, orders, and/or operations. Full schedule print-outs are available but it may be difficult to compare schedules by doing this as the schedules may be very large and very different. OPS provides a simple method of comparing schedules based on criteria determined by the manufacturer. It is therefore a simple matter to compare schedules.

Firm and Nonfirm Orders

The production planners know which orders are actual firm orders (usually customer orders) and which are nonfirm (usually forecast orders). This enables them to ensure that firm orders are least affected when modifications need to be done.

Actual vs. Planned

OPS reports which orders have been completed, which are currently being manufactured, and which are still pending. It is able to compare actual times (when work has been completed) against planned times. This enables the production planners to easily recognize any differences between how long they believed orders would take compared to how long they actually did take. They then, if necessary, adjust any "base" production or processing (manufacturing) times which may have been inaccurate.

Work Tickets

Work tickets are produced by the scheduler to formats suitable to the manufacturer. Once a schedule is generated, work tickets and any other desired travel documents are produced within minutes. This is not only convenient, it is also necessary if a schedule is changed suddenly. The production staff are notified quickly through formal means (work tickets, etc.).

Realistic Customer Times

Potential customers often like to know when orders will be completed if those orders were given to the manufacturer. The sales staff need to be able to tell them but production may not be able to give a better than approximate answer to sales. With OPS, production is able to give sales an accurate answer. This is done by simply including the potential order into the existing manufacturing requirements and printing a "what if" schedule.

Customer Progress Enquiries

It is not unusual for customers to phone and enquire about their orders. With OPS, they are told almost immediately where their orders are in the manufacturing shop and how these orders are going compared to schedule. Indeed, if anything happens to affect the progress of orders (such as machine breakdowns, staff problems, nonavailability of raw material, etc.) customers are told well in advance that their orders may be late and how late they will be, even if their orders haven't been started. This enables the customers to put into place their own contingency plans.

Planners Now Plan

The computerized scheduler frees the production planners from the tedious and repetitious tasks of generating schedules. It allows them to plan, monitor, supervise, and communicate with sales/marketing/purchasing a lot more factually and often. It was for these skills they were presumably employed; more than mere human calculators.

Overall Dollar Savings

Large dollar savings have been made because of using the computerized scheduler. Users of the computerized scheduler have made savings orders of magnitude greater than they anticipated because of benefits (due to the scheduler) that they had not envisaged.

SCHEDULE BASED MANUFACTURING

The SBM philosophy grew from interactive real-time shop floor scheduling (such as OPS above) in much the same way that the MRP II philosophy grew from MRP. MRP (materials) added rough capacity planning (resources) to become MRP II. Material requirements were added to OPS (resources) to become SBM. SBM is based on the following facts:

> Inventory (raw, WIP, and finished) is a function of resources, shop floor loading, and time.

> Resources are a function of materials, resources, shop floor loading, and time.

> Manufacturing is a function of materials, resources, shop floor loading, and time which must be considered simultaneously, not independently.

The creation of the SBM philosophy from OPS was driven commercially rather than academically. It occurred during the final years of the author's 15-year industrial career, before returning to academe. It is interesting to note that similar ideas were being developed at the same time by Professor N. Hastings and his various coworkers. Whilst the philosophy was the same, the computing tools were somewhat different.

When SBM is implemented, jobs (or shop orders) are submitted directly to the scheduler which generates a production schedule based on available actual resources so capacity planning is no longer necessary. Capacity reports are printed if and when required. Both forecast and actual jobs are submitted to the scheduler thus removing the need for a traditional MPS. Material requirements reports are produced based on actual lead times, not estimated static lead times so traditional MRP is also not required. SBM was designed to increase productivity by eliminating both the horizontal and vertical separation of MRP II.

EXTRA IMPROVEMENTS FROM SBM

SBM is simple, accurate, and timely. It considers material and resources simultaneously. Implementing SBM gives the following improvements in addition to those given by using interactive real-time scheduling tools such as OPS:

Material and Resource Requirements are coupled.

Accuracy.

Traditional MRP is not required.

Traditional MPS is not required.

Traditional Capacity Planning is not required.

Easier to learn and maintain.

Less manual intervention.

Smaller computer requirements.

Two Case Studies

The two companies used in this comparison were using MRP II (Before) prior to the introduction of interactive scheduling (After).

	Before	*After*
Manufacturer 1		
Raw Materials Stock	$700,000	$5,000
White Metal Stock	$500,000	$50,000
Finished Goods Stock	$8,000,000	Less than $500,000
Service Staff	8 people	1 person
Manufacturing Lead Time	5.5 weeks	1.5 weeks
Number Shop Orders in Factory	700	300

	Before	*After*
Work-in-Process	720 pallets	380 pallets
Stockouts	220 SKU's	10 SKU's
Late Jobs	Almost all	Very few, if any
Manufacturer 2		
Production Planning Time	12 days/month	30 minutes/day
Customer Service Level	74%	96%
Savings in Inventory		Over $2,000,000 to date
Shop Floor Information	Inaccurate	Accurate

Chapter 7

Finite Capacity Scheduling Implementation

The best way to have a good idea is to have many of them.
—LINUS PAULING

The implementation of a production scheduling and control system can be quite complex. This chapter will take you through the various stages of the implementation plan. You will need to identify the stage that you are currently at and fit yourself into this planning process. Then you can work toward a totally integrated production planning, scheduling, and control system.

THE SUPPORT SYSTEMS

The first step in the development of a production planning system is to identify what the critical resources are and establish systems to manage these resources. These resources include:

Inventory/materials.

Labor/personnel.

Machinery/tools.

Facilities.

Next we need to develop appropriate information support systems around those items that are considered to be critical to the operation. First and foremost is the inventory control system. The inventory system manages inventory receipts and issues, accounts for inspection, and tracks on-hand balances. Without an accurate inventory count, it would be difficult to establish meaningful control of the inventory resource.

A key piece of the materials resource database is the bill of materials. This database will track all the component requirements of the parts produced in the production process. Although MRP systems determine what is required, they are not capable of determining at what time in the process the material will be required. This function will be calculated by the FCS system.

Implementation of an FCS system requires acknowledgment that the MRP master schedule can be run on a regular basis if desired by the user; however, the only value will be for rough cut planning. The FCS scheduling module will replace all MRP scheduling functions. If this is not understood and accepted, the FCS implementation will be a failure. A review of the logic of MRP and FCS scheduling will be useful to ensure that the implementation is off to a good start.

Both MRP and FCS systems create routings to define the sequence of events through the plant. The routings are very similar in appearance, but the dynamics of scheduling are quite different. MRP systems assume the process time for each part is constant based on predetermined standards. These standards include estimated queue times and do not produce effective schedules that can be followed. FCS routings do not include estimated queue time assumptions. Rather, FCS systems calculate the actual queue time for each part at each work center to the minute based on current demand. The degree of calculation error in FCS schedules is a function of input error, and this error should be minimal. The FCS calculations are based on current conditions, including work order demand, capacity, and constraints. Work center queue times vary dramatically based on order mix, particularly in job shop environments. Flow shops also have varying cycle times albeit they tend to be less dynamic than job shops. Although queue times vary to a lesser degree in flow shops, do not expect MRP schedules to be accurate enough to be followed; they will rapidly diverge from reality and require frequent updating and rescheduling. Users of MRP are so dependent on the tracking system that many refer to the tracking system when asked about MRP scheduling.

Defining *maximum* resource availability by work center is the same for both MRP and FCS. Each resource has a maximum limit; for example, if three machines exist in a work center, you cannot make simultaneous use of more than three machines at any moment.

We alluded earlier to the problem of measuring capacity, and this is a good place to elaborate on why there has been so much diversity about capacity measurement. Defining capacity limitation at any specific moment is quite easy for a single resource; the total number of machines in a work center is a hard constraint. If, however, you have three machines and run two shifts and have only one operator on the second shift who can operate the machines, the total usable capacity is different for MRP or FCS using the data shown in Table 7.1.

The example in Table 7.1 is a classic multiple resource constraint: The actual capacity available for the machine work center is constrained by operators available.

If management elects to add an operator on the second shift for one month to relieve a short-term bottleneck, it would alter the actual capacity available for that month. You can easily see that neither MRP nor manually calculated capacity values will be very accurate since availability is dynamic. Availability depends on accurate scheduling to determine utilization and availability. To produce valid capacity measurement for this example demands a system that is capable of evaluating dynamic loading conditions and does not violate constraints. Multiplying the resources times the hours per day that they are perceived to be available does not give the actual capacity available when multiple resource constraints are imposed.

The compound conditions of variable resources by shift, multiple resource constraints, setup minimization, and other dynamic complexities add perplexity to the process of measuring capacity. This supports the statement by C. J. McNair

Table 7.1   Resource Availability of a
Machine Work Center That Requires an
Operator

Resources Available	Shift 1	Shift 2
Machines	3	3
Operators	3	1
Actual machine availability	3	1

and Richard Vangermeersch, "Capacity cost management is a journey, not a destination."

For example, we need to identify the timing—the amount of labor and machinery resources that are available, and when they become available. In MRP, this capacity information is used after production schedules are generated. The MRP-generated schedule is revalidated against capacity using a Capacity Requirements Planning (CRP) module that *attempts* to adjust for the capacity mismatches generated by the MRP schedule. This is the major difference between MRP and FCS schedules. FCS generates workable schedules that don't require realignment with capacity. Additionally, since the alignment occurs as an afterthought in the CRP system, it never produces a feasible solution.

Planning and Scheduling

Most FCS systems are installed to interface with an existing MRP system and there is a perception that the MRP routings can be downloaded to the FCS system. This concept is flawed. Although the static routings appear very similar, the amount of routing detail required for FCS exceeds what is available in the MRP routings. The interest and desire to download routings from MRP to FCS is perceived as saving dual input. Several options exist. The MRP routing file can be revised to include all the data; however, this is not as easy as it might appear. Good scheduling demands accurate data, and FCS systems include consistency checking to eliminate data input errors. The software development required to implement this function into an existing MRP system is not economical. The alternative is to enter the data in the FCS system and upload the necessary data to the MRP system.

This installation debate needs to be addressed early to avoid wasting time downstream. If you find that the required data is available in the MRP system, either you have an exceptional MRP system or the FCS vendor software is less sophisticated than you may desire.

With the support systems in place, we can move forward and begin the interface of MRP to FCS. Figure 7.1 shows the implementation of MRP and FCS in parallel to indicate that, as discussed in earlier chapters, an iterative process is necessary to coordinate material and capacity. The coordination is accomplished by bouncing between these two systems. It is seldom necessary for more than two iterations.

Which system runs first is not very important. Until both have processed at least one pass it is not possible to determine what adjustments are necessary to eliminate conflicts. Most MRP users will naturally have an inclination to run MRP, then FCS. This is not necessarily the best approach,

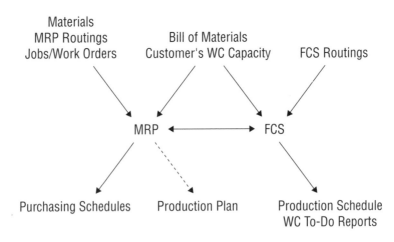

Figure 7.1 MRP-FCS Schedule Generation.

though. As a general rule, the two systems will converge with the least user effort if the system that has more constraints is processed first. Capacity is most often the greatest constraint, so we suggest running the FCS schedule first, then the MRP material system—unless you have concrete evidence that material is more constrained than capacity.

Some vendors now claim to calculate material and capacity concurrently. We cannot validate these claims; however, we do know that work is progressing in this direction at multiple companies.

With an established implementation of the MRP environment, we are now ready to migrate to the next step, to implement the FCS system. This is seen in Figure 7.2 where

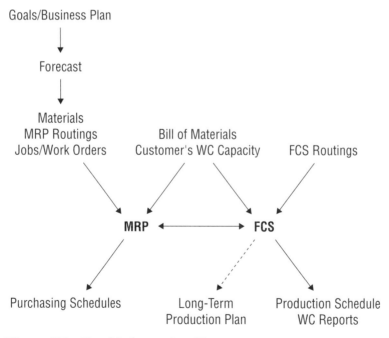

Figure 7.2 Total Information Flow.

each step in the planning and scheduling process is built on the information found in the previous step.

The flow of information when FCS and MRP systems are interfaced is different from the flow of information using only an MRP system. MRP master schedule, rough cut capacity (RCC), and aggregate production schedule (APS) are not shown in the process. Figure 7.1 includes production plan as a dotted line to indicate that it can be run if desired. Many companies will continue to use the MRP long-term planning facility; however, the FCS system can also be used to produce long-term planning and the results will be more accurate since resource utilization will be based on finite capacity.

With the integrated manufacturing planning and scheduling system in place, we can now grow the system into a Manufacturing Resources Planning (MRP II) environment. This jump integrates the production planning systems with the costing and accounting systems and the sales support systems. This can be seen in Figure 7.3.

Enterprise Resource Planning (ERP) adds another dimension to the MRP II environment. MRP II treats each factory as an independent environment requiring its own planning and scheduling, while ERP removes the factory isolation barriers and treats the entire organization as a collection of integrated factories. This integration offers information interchange and big picture planning. It creates an internal supply chain network within the organization. In Figure 7.4 we see this by the Interfactory Logistics Planning interface with the MRP and FCS systems. This piece decides what is going to be produced in each facility based on the overall planning of the organization. The logistics planning affects the customer interface as well as the vendor interfaces.

An additional piece that ERP offers is expanded infor-

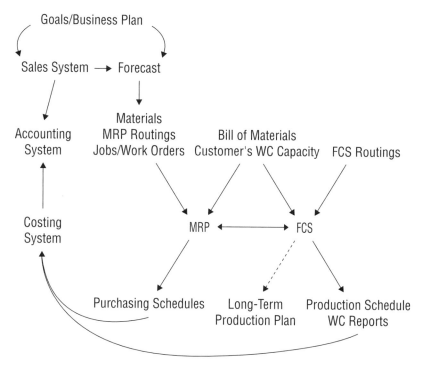

Figure 7.3 MRP II Integration.

mation integration. ERP integrates the engineering information and makes it accessible to the production floor, to vendors, and to customers. Actual drawings can now be available online to anyone involved in the product being produced.

Supply Chain Management (SCM) takes ERP principles outside of the organization. The objective of SCM is to integrate the entire network of planning and scheduling information from the vendor's vendor through to the customer's customer. Resources are planned within the defined constraints. As a result, cycle times are compacted, service levels are improved, and inventory levels are reduced.

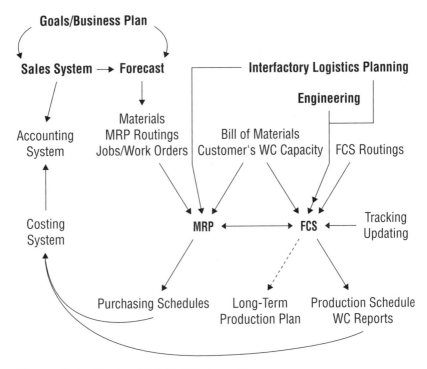

Figure 7.4   Revised MRP II Integration.

Value Chain Management (VCM) is the next enhancement beyond SCM. VCM expands even further on SCM by integrating the efficiency of all resources, including financial. With VCM the profitability of the entire supply chain is investigated for all elements, particularly focusing on the elimination of financial waste. For example, Dell Computer Corporation was able to eliminate its retail and distribution intermediary and sell directly to the consumer through Internet marketing techniques. The result is a saving at all levels of the supply chain.

IMPLEMENTATION PLANNING

Just like planning a factory, the implementation of an FCS system requires the planning of resources. The key areas of resource planning include:

Software planning.

Hardware planning.

Implementation scheduling.

Training planning.

Conversion planning.

The best planning schedules include graphic output, usually in a Gantt chart format where all the steps and time lines of the FCS implementation project are projected out in time. This schedule should be visible to everyone involved in or affected by the implementation. A sample chart can be seen in Table 7.2. This diagram is incomplete, representing only a format for planning. Implementation could take anywhere from 50 to 100 weeks. Numerous project management systems are available that are helpful in managing the planning function for implementation.

Another critical piece in implementation planning is the definition of responsibility for each task. Once again, Table 7.3 attempts to give an example of possible assignments.

SOFTWARE SELECTION GUIDELINES

Organizations like APICS offer annual directories that do a feature/function and price comparison of software packages

Table 7.2 Conversion Gantt Chart

Activity												Week								
	1	2	3	4	5	6	7	8	9	10	11	12	13	14	15	16	17	18	19	20
Define goals/business plan	*	*																		
Establish forecast, RCC, and APS		*	*	*																
Define MPS			*	*	*	*	*	*	*	*	*	*								
Training													*	*	*	*	*	*	*	*
Develop inventory system	*	*	*	*	*	*	*	*	*	*	*	*								
Develop routings					*	*	*	*	*	*	*	*								
Develop bills of materials	*	*	*	*	*	*	*	*	*	*	*	*								

Week

Activity	1	2	3	4	5	6	7	8	9	10	11	12	13	14	15	16	17	18	19	20
Develop bills of machinery					*	*	*	*	*	*	*	*								
Develop actual operation times					*	*	*	*	*	*	*	*	*	*	*	*				
Define capacities									*	*	*	*	*							
Install MRP											*	*	*	*	*	*	*	*	*	*
Install FCS											*	*	*	*	*	*	*	*	*	*
Integrate MRP II																			*	
*Integrate engineering																				
Develop logistics plan																				
Integrate ERP																				

Table 7.3 Task Assignment Chart

Activity	Primary Assignment	Secondary Assignment
Define goals/ business plan	Strategic management	
Establish forecast, RCC, and APS	Tactical management	
Define MPS	Production management	Materials management
Develop inventory system	Storeroom	Information systems group
Develop routings	Engineering	Shop floor
Develop bills of materials	Engineering	
Develop bills of machinery	Engineering	
Develop actual operation times	Engineering	Shop floor
Define capacities	Shop floor department	
Install MRP	Production planning group	Information systems group
Install FCS	Production scheduling	Information systems group
Integrate MRP II department	Production management	Accounting
Integrate engineering	Engineering	Information systems group
Develop logistics plan	Production management	Materials management
Integrate ERP	Tactical management	Materials management

that are available. This is a starting point in determining systems that are on the market. From this directory you can select vendors that appear to fit within your criteria. Then you can contact the vendor and get additional details about the software product. Remember the key principle of software analysis:

Always compare vendors by applying your actual live data, and never base your analysis on the vendor's demo data.

For FCS, a feature/function list is often in the directory; however, it is seldom realistic. Most directories produce a matrix of features and request the vendors to complete the questionnaire. When this is the process, you will not get a true picture. Vendors are generous in stating their capabilities, and these guidelines grow out-of-date quickly.

SUMMARY

The implementation process of any system, more than the quality of the system itself, determines the degree of success or failure of the system. A key principle here is:

> No matter how good a system is, if the users don't have ownership of the system it will fail. Similarly, even if the system is marginal, if the users have ownership of the system it will be deemed a success.

Therefore, careful implementation planning is critical to the success of FCS.

Part III

MANAGEMENT STYLES

Chapter 8

The Role of Management

For a conscious being, to exist is to change, to change is to mature, to mature is to go on creating oneself endlessly.
—HENRI BERGSON, French philosopher

INTRODUCTION

As a farmer was walking through one of his fields one day, he came across a frightened baby eagle that was clumsily stumbling, trying to run to escape. It looked as though its parents had abandoned it, and it was too young to be able to fly. Feeling sorry for the little bird, the farmer picked it up, took it back to the farm, and placed it with a flock of baby turkeys that had recently hatched. The eaglet grew up eating turkey food, walking like a turkey, talking with turkeys, learning from turkeys, and thinking that being a turkey was the best thing to be.

One day the farmer decided the eaglet was old enough

to return to the wild on its own, and so he took it out to the field to show it that it could fly. He picked it up and threw it up in the air. But the eagle, still thinking like a turkey, fell back to the ground. The farmer tried again, throwing the bird higher. He reasoned that if the eagle saw that it hurt to hit the ground, it might be forced to spread its wings and fly. But again, the eagle hit the ground. The farmer repeated this process over and over for several days until one day the eagle, tired of hitting the ground, spread its wings and realized it wasn't a turkey after all. It could fly. It was an eagle.

Many of us have been raised like managerial turkeys, thinking that the way we were taught to do things is the best way and that we shouldn't question anything. It is time to quit falling to the ground and to realize that we are eagles. We may hit the ground a few times before we realize this, but we can be eagles, and we can fly.

MANAGEMENT STYLES

As with any goal, the first step is defining our target. What is it we would like to be as a manager? Next we identify where we currently are. Then, using this information we design a travel plan getting us from where we are to where we want to end up. To do this we focus on the tools that are available to us.[1]

Initially we will review some of the different types of management styles that exist so we can figure out what we want to be and where we currently are. There are several

---

[1] Parts of this section are taken from the book *World Class Manager*, by Gerhard Plenert (Rocklin, CA: Prima Publishing, 1995).

types of managers, and there are numerous ways to categorize them. For example, there is the sunrise manager who has a view toward the future, as opposed to the sunset manager who fights fires in the here and now. We often think of the sunrise manager as the dreamer and the sunset manager as the workaholic. Are you a sunrise manager or a sunset manager?

Another way to classify managers is to consider their attitudes toward their subordinates. The two extremes are the authoritarian manager and participative manager. Authoritarian managers are typified by being secretive, having their fingers in everything that happens, always having the final word, and telling, rather than asking. This type of manager is often referred to as the Theory-X manager.

Participative managers value employee opinions. They spend more time listening than talking during a meeting. They look for ideas from the bottom, realizing that employees have the best understanding of day-to-day operations. This type of manager is often referred to as a Theory-Y manager.[2]

There is a second type of participative manager. These managers tend to empower employees to make their own decisions and to implement their own ideas. This form of participative manager is referred to as the Theory-Z manager.[3] In

---

[2] For more information about Theory-X and Theory-Y managers, including some very interesting examples, read the book *The Human Side of the Enterprise*, by Douglas McGregor (New York: McGraw-Hill, 1985).

[3] Theory-Z management is explained nicely, including examples, in the following book and article:

Pascale, Richard Tanner, and Anthony G. Athos, *The Art of Japanese Management*, New York: Warner Books, 1982.

Joiner, Charles W., Jr., "Making the 'Z' Concept Work," *Sloan Management Review*, Spring 1985, pp. 57–63.

this management style we switch the top-down decision-making process that is characteristic of the Theory-X and even Theory-Y management style to a bottom-up decision-making process characteristic of the Japanese management style. In the Theory-Z style we are heavily involved in teaming. Managers take on the role of facilitator. Theory-Z managers keep their teams focused and present them with areas that need consideration and evaluation, but let the team make their own improvement decisions. So, are you a Theory-X, Theory-Y, or Theory-Z manager?

A third way to classify managers uses the Five Cs. These are cash, crisis, conflict, cool, and change. Cash managers focus on costs and budgets and have probably come through the accounting or finance ranks. This type of manager tends to be risk-averse and looks toward stability rather than opportunity. Crisis managers believe you shouldn't fix anything that isn't broken. This style of manager, like the cash manager, strives toward stability, looking at problems as disruptions that need to be conquered, rather than as opportunities for future improvements. Conflict managers look at the workplace as a battlefield of competing players. They always feel the need to take and maintain the upper hand through whatever means are necessary. Control is the primary tool of power, and intimidation is the primary motivating force. Cool managers believe the work force is best motivated by giving it whatever it wants. These managers try to bribe their way into the hearts of their children, which is how they view their employees. Change managers search for challenges in competitiveness. These managers thrive on positive, goal-focused changes, seeing them as the opportunities that make work exciting. Have you identified yourself yet?

A last but important method for classifying a manager is to compare the boss to the leader. A boss directs employee traffic, whereas a leader guides the way using appropriate examples and by stepping out into the traffic in front of the employees. Bosses manage, but leaders tend to head out and search for a difference.[4]

> Insecure managers create complexity. Real leaders don't need clutter.
> —JOHN F. WELCH, JR., chairman and CEO, General Electric[5]

Now it's time for you to:

1. Identify what type of manager you would like to be.

2. Identify how you would currently classify yourself.

You need to integrate the different types of management style in order to define your own personal style.

---

[4] Many good articles discuss the role of leaders in a changing, growing organization. For example:

Senge, Peter M., "The Leader's New Work: Building Learning Organizations," *Sloan Management Review*, Fall 1990, pp. 7–23. This article focuses on the need for an organization to be "continuously learning" through leadership.

Kotter, John P., "What Leaders Really Do," *Harvard Business Review*, May–June 1990, pp. 103–111. This article stresses that "good management controls complexity; effective leadership produces useful change." The article observes that "management controls people by pushing them in the right direction; leadership motivates them by satisfying basic human needs." This article offers three interesting leadership examples and is worth checking into just for the chance to read about the examples (American Express, Eastman Kodak, and Procter & Gamble).

[5] Jack Welch's opinions about what makes a good manager ("business leader" is the term Jack prefers) are discussed in an interesting article: "Speed, Simplicity, Self-Confidence: An Interview with Jack Welch," by Noel Tichy and Ram Charan, *Harvard Business Review*, Sept.–Oct. 1989, pp. 112–120.

What type of manager do you think you are? Are you a Theory-X/sunset/cash manager, who would be a bean-counting, bossy firefighter telling everyone what to do, how to do it, and when to do it, and insisting that no one does anything until directed? Or are you a Theory-Y/sunrise/cool leader who loves everyone, likes to show rather than tell everyone how to do a job, and shares schemes of grandeur with employees?

A world-class manager (WCM) is a sunrise/Theory-Z/ change leader. A WCM should be a:

Sunrise manager—looking for the better way, with a long-term orientation.

Theory-Z manager—having employees involved with and guiding the business process through participative and empowered team efforts.

Change manager—guiding a dynamic, evolving business organism that capitalizes on change opportunities.

Leader—being a character-building, motivational example.

A world-class manager views the future as an opportunity, and the here and now as adequate for the past, but just not good enough for the future. This manager views all aspects of the enterprise—systems, production philosophies, and even management styles that were in existence 20 to 30 years ago—as wholly deficient for today and especially inadequate for the future.

By their very nature, world-class managers are risk takers, since change always involves risk. Additionally, the long-term perspective of world-class managers often makes them unpopular in the short run. World-class managers enjoy the excitement of being leading-edge innovators, despite the occasional failures they will suffer on this risky management road.

WHY IS CHANGE NECESSARY?

There are several reasons for change. The first reason is competition, whether from domestic or foreign competitors. We need to improve to stay ahead of our competitors. Another reason for change is to take advantage of technological advancements, such as automation or computerization. Still another reason for change is the changing habits of our customers.

There are numerous models for implementing change, from the slow and systematic, such as Total Quality Management (TQM), to the fast and radical such as Process Reengineering (PR). There are models that motivate change through their measurement process, and there are measurement systems that discourage change. Correctly implemented change models give us an entirely new focus on what change can do for us. When we manage change, rather than letting change manage us, our focus becomes global, technology-oriented, flexible, and customer-responsive.

Innovation is seldom rewarded, and only in the case of extreme success is the innovator thanked for his or her risk taking. The result is a fear of innovation and change, like a change to FCS. A world-class manager focuses on the opportunities rather than the problems. Problems and errors bring the opportunities to our attention, but the WCM will resist solving the problem and will prefer to focus on the opportunity for change. Alone, these statements sound idealistic.

However, what this really means is that problems or errors occur because there is some basic need that is not being taken care of properly.

We need to establish an environment of motivated innovation within our organizations by removing the fear of change. We need to *focus* on innovation in our enterprises, and this can be achieved only with properly motivated changes. One of the best examples of innovative change is the Toyota Just-in-Time production system. Just-in-Time (JIT) is a production planning philosophy developed in Japan that focuses on waste minimization through inventory reductions. But JIT didn't exist before being developed by the Toyota Motor Corporation. It wasn't copied; it was "innoveered" (the Disney Company's term for innovation engineering). Here's a brief summary of the story.

It was post–World War II and Japan was trying to rebuild its industry. The Japanese tried copying Western (primarily United States) production methodologies, which were considered the best in the world, but they soon encountered four problems:

1. The Japanese lacked the cash flow to finance the large in-process inventory levels required by the U.S. batch-oriented production systems.

2. The Japanese lacked the land space to build large U.S.-style factories.

3. The Japanese didn't have the natural resource accessibility that the United States had.

4. Japan had labor excess rather than a labor shortage, which meant that labor efficiency systems weren't very valuable.

The Japanese innoveered these problems into opportunities. They realized that their competitive problem was a process problem, not a product problem. They proceeded to copy product technology, and worked diligently to innovate *process* technology oriented around materials efficiency rather than labor efficiency. The result was the flow-through JIT production methodology for which Toyota has become famous. But Toyota will be the first to admit that it wasn't easy. Toyota officials scoff at U.S. attempts to copy JIT after two or three years of implementation. They will readily say it took them 30 years to develop JIT. But they got there by one innoveering change at a time.

The result was that the Japanese built smaller factories (about one-third the size of their counterparts in the United States) in which ideally the only materials were those on which work was currently being done.[6] In this way inventory levels were kept low, investment in in-process inventory was at a minimum, and the investment in purchased natural resources was quickly turned around so that additional materials were purchased.[7] The focus was on materials (inventory) efficiency rather than labor efficiency.

---

[6] In reality, the Japanese work with single-digit batch sizes (one to nine units), whereas U.S. batch sizes can range in the hundreds of units. For each batch, only one item in the batch is worked on at a time; the rest of the batch is inventory. Therefore, a batch of 100 units creates a continuous, ongoing inventory of 99 units. Unfortunately, the batch is often not being worked on and is just idle inventory. This batch size difference between the United States and Japan creates a tremendous difference in inventory levels.

[7] Numerous books detail the Toyota production philosophy JIT:

Shingo, Shigeo, *Study of the Toyota Production System from the Industrial Engineering Viewpoint*, Tokyo: Japanese Management Association, 1981. Shingo has worked with Toyota and has an insider's viewpoint.

Wantuck, Kenneth A., *Just in Time for America*, Milwaukee: The Forum, Ltd., 1989.

In the United States we are past the point of trying to copy Japan. We need to innoveer beyond what we can copy from anyone if we are to stay competitive. As long as we are playing copycat, the best we can ever do is to get caught up; and that's just not good enough![8] The only way we can get ahead is by innoveering. The Japanese will stay ahead only as long as we, by focusing on copying rather than innoveering, allow them to. And the key to innoveered, innovative change in manufacturing scheduling is found in FCS.

Imagination is more important than knowledge.

—ALBERT EINSTEIN

GOAL SETTING

Goals give purpose and direction to what we are doing. We need to focus on a clearly defined target in order to get direction in what we are trying to accomplish. In the development of a goal we initially need to establish goals at the highest levels of the organization. These goals are then filtered and distributed to lower levels of the organization as subgoals and charters. Starting from the top, we develop these goals in the following stages:

---

[8] This concept of innovating yourself out ahead rather than copying someone else is the theme of another book by Gerhard Plenert, *International Management and Production: Survival Techniques for Corporate America* (Blue Ridge Summit, PA: Tab Professional and Reference Books, 1990).

1. Defining the corporate values.

2. Defining the core competencies.

3. The vision.

4. The mission.

5. Strategic initiatives.

6. The strategy.

7. The plan of operation.

The first step is not really a goal as much as it is an introspective look at what the organization stands for. The corporate values are set down in a value statement that describes the uncompromisable ethical behavior that everyone in the organization is expected to live up to. Similarly, the core competencies are an introspective look at what the organization is good at—the organization's competitive edge. Are you good at each phase—sourcing, manufacturing, distribution, retailing, and customer service? Probably not.

After defining the values and core competencies, we use these to start developing the goal structure. The first step is the development of top-level goals that define the organization as forward-looking. To become a visionary company you need two things:

1. A guiding philosophy and value system, a vision.

2. A challenging short-term goal or mission that quantifies the vision.

In each stage of the goal development process we find more detail than at the level before it. For example, the vision statement is one or two sentences of where the enterprise is going. The vision defines the enterprise's sense of purpose, its reason for being, and its guiding philosophy. A vision builds unity throughout the organization. It doesn't have to be long, but it has to give the organization purpose. The vision should provide employees with a clear image that they can identify with. For example:

> To make people happy.
> —WALT DISNEY

Unlike the undefined, timeless vision statement, the mission statement provides a defined goal for the enterprise that is aimed at the vision. The mission has a definite, measurable goal and should be date stamped with a finish line. One example is:

> Achieving the goal, before this decade is out, of landing a man on the moon and returning him safely to earth.
> —PRESIDENT JOHN F. KENNEDY, 1962

The vision and mission statements are defined by the strategic management levels, which include the CEO and the board of directors. The next stage, strategy development, is performed primarily by the tactical management functions, which include the CEO and vice president (VP) level of the organization. In the strategic phase of goal setting, we start by defining a set of about five strategic initiatives. These are five statements of planned accomplishment, similar to five mission statements. However, they focus on five strategic areas of accomplishment that the organization will have to achieve in order to accomplish the mission. For example, in President Kennedy's mission we would want to define a technology strategic initiative, one for human resources, another for financing, and still another for international integration.

The next stage of goal development is to use the strategic initiatives to develop a strategy. The strategy identifies and quantifies goals for each strategic operating area and focuses on bringing that operating area in focus with the mission of the enterprise. A strategy is developed for each year of the mission. In each of these years, a strategy is designed for:

➢ People:
  First employees:
    Education and training,
    Empowerment,
    Teamwork,
    Organizational structure,
    Staff functions.
  Then customers:
    Involvement.
  Then vendors:
    Supply chain integration.

➢ Integration:
  Elimination of barriers,
  Information.

➢ Globalization.

➤ Measurement:
  Internal performance:
  Quality,
  Productivity,
  Efficiency.
  External performance:
  Adding value to society,
  Customer-perceived quality,
  Market share.
  Internal factors:
  Capacity,
  Equipment,
  Operational performance.
  External factors:
  Competition,
  Economic conditions,
  Government regulation.
  Focused.
  Motivational.

➤ Continuous change process focused on adding value:
  Elimination of waste,
  Identifying strengths and weaknesses,
  Identifying opportunities and threats.

➤ Time-based competition:
  Time-to-market strategy.

➤ Technology:
  Funding,
  Facilities and equipment,
  Planning and scheduling (FCS).

World-class strategies focus on world-class competitiveness. Some of the competitive trends for the next decade include:

➤ Rapid change in technology and markets.

➤ More competitors globally.

➤ Increased emphasis on globalization.

➤ Environmental consciousness.

➤ Decentralization.

➤ Shrinking company sizes (strategic alliances).

➤ Closer links to customers and suppliers.

➤ Competitive emphasis on:
  Cost reduction,
  Customer-oriented quality improvement,
  Flexibility a priority,
  Time-to-market responsiveness.

➤ Borderless companies:
  Removal of departmentalization.[9]

The last step in the goal-setting process is the plan of operation. This is the operating plan for each strategic area for the current year, detailing how each area will achieve its strategy. The plan of operation requires a detailed tactical plan, with budgets and operational planning details by

---

[9] Taken from Chapter 4 of the book *World Class Manager* by Gerhard Plenert, (Rocklin, CA: Prima Publishing, 1995).

functional area, for executing the strategy in the short term (over the next year).

In order to discuss goals effectively, we also need to discuss the types of goals that exist and their characteristics.[10] It is also possible to have secondary goals, but they need to complement, not draw away from, the primary goal.

> Where there is no vision, the people perish.
> —Proverbs 29:18

Types of Goals

In the United States, culture and tradition have led companies to grow accustomed to the idea that there is only one correct goal for a business enterprise—financial. However, this goal is in the minority when taking an international perspective. Internationally there are four major groupings of goals:

1. Financial.
2. Operational.
3. Employee-based.
4. Customer-based.

Financial goals include, for example, to increase profits, decrease costs, increase sales, increase return on investment, increase return on net assets, and/or increase financial ratios. Financial goals tend to be shortsighted because they often focus on quarterly or annual results. But, in spite of the shortsighted negatives, financial goals can, and often are, used to

---

[10] See Chapter 3 of the book *World Class Manager* by Gerhard Plenert (Rocklin, CA: Prima Publishing, 1995) for a more in-depth explanation of these concepts.

effect positive growth and change. The key to success seems to be in the realization that long-term visions and missions are not achieved when they are restricted by short-term measures that don't focus on the long-term goals.

Operational goals have caught on in some parts of Europe. Operational goals tend to be more long-term than financial goals. Additionally, achieving operational goals tends to have, as a by-product, the achievement of financial objectives. Operational goals include, for example, improved quality, improved productivity, reduced inventory, increased throughput, reduced scrap, and improved customer service level. It is easy to see how achieving each of these goals would improve profits. Additionally, these goals tend to be nonconflicting.

Employee permanence and stability is an important goal that is used quite often in Japan. The primary reason for the popularity of this goal is that it supports a participative relationship with the employees, rather than the authoritarian one. But there is a lot of misunderstanding about what this goal means and doesn't mean. For example, it doesn't mean that the company should ignore profitability, any more than a successful, profit-oriented company can ignore its employees. It simply means that successful, happy employees create a successful, happy company.

Federal Express, from its inception, has put its people first both because it is right to do so and because it is good business as well. Our corporate philosophy is succinctly stated: People-Service-Profit (P-S-P).
—FREDERICK W. SMITH, chairman and CEO, Federal Express

A customer-based goal often gets confused with a quality-based goal. Quality is a strategy for achieving any of the goals. But quality itself is an operational goal. To be customer-oriented you would need to spend time with your customer at your customer's location, and your customer would spend time with you and your employees at your location. You would share, discuss, interact, learn, and create ideas (innovate) together. The customer would be an integral part of your planning circle.

Financial and operational goals are easy to measure. It's all in the data and can be displayed neatly on a graph. Working with employees and customers is vague and not quite as quantifiable. Maybe that's why Americans shy away from employee- and customer-based goals.

Characteristics of Good Goals

The typical business plan of a company reads like a wish list of all good things and is totally worthless. Having lots of business goals is as useful as not having any, if they are not focused on a common vision. The goals soon get in each other's way. Goal setting should also not be a process of setting high goals to drive employees to unrealistic ends. Nor should the desire for goal attainment result in a compromise of easy-to-attain steps. A good target should be realistic and attainable. Specifically, there are several characteristics that all goals should have (most goals do not have all of these characteristics, but you should try to include as many as possible):

1. Participatively created by and matched to the employees.

2. Shared.

3. Nonconflicting.

4. Designed to allow for and encourage change.

5. Simple but not simplistic.

6. Precise.

7. Measurable.

8. Uncompromised.

9. Focused.

10. Achievable yet challenging.

MOTIVATION

World-class managers motivate goal-directed changes. For example, in the implementation of FCS, this means:

1. Commitment from top management.

2. Participation from all levels of the organization in the selection of the FCS system.

3. Organization-wide involvement in the selection, training, and implementation of an FCS system.

4. Goal-focused, team-based project plan for conversion and implementation.

Without the world-class approach, the implementation of FCS—or any other major change of this type in the organization—cannot succeed.

SUMMARY

This chapter has focused on:

Defining a management style.

Focusing on change.

Establishing meaningful goals.

Motivating employees toward the goals.

Any system, especially an FCS system, requires these steps to be in place in order for an implementation to be successful. The next chapter discusses how these goals are utilized to motivate focused employee responses.

I'm always doing what I can't do yet in order to learn how to do it.
—VINCENT VAN GOGH

The Measurement
of Performance

*Too many people prefer
the misery of uncertainty
over the pain of change.*

INTRODUCTION

In the Gobi desert there is a regiment of troops. Their primary function is to keep the railroad tracks clear of sand. The purpose of the railroad is to deliver food and supplies to the troops. Does this seem strange? Often we become comfortable doing things the way they have always been done, never questioning why. Like soldiers in the Gobi desert, traditional measurement systems (such as labor efficiency or productivity measures) not only are ineffective, but they are usually a waste, and they are often destructive.

In designing or selecting a manufacturing scheduling system, we soon learn that it is impossible to incorporate a shop floor system without some measures of performance. These are needed for several reasons:

➤ Validation of process improvements.

➤ Employee motivation.

➤ Goal achievement.

In this chapter we will consider some of the critical elements of a successful measurement system. We will start with a review of the measurement-motivation relationship. This will be followed with a discussion of several measurement options. The chapter will end with a comparison of the various measurement methodologies and how they relate to FCS.

THE MEASUREMENT-MOTIVATION RELATIONSHIP

The authors feel that the key to successful performance in any system is not in the procedures, like ISO certification or MRP scheduling. Rather, successful shop floor performance is achieved by establishing meaningful structured measurement systems focused on results rather than on data collection. With this idea in mind Gerhard Plenert received an APICS grant for research focused on the relationship between motivation and measurement,[1] with the belief that:

---

[1] The details of this research were published in an APICS Education and Research Foundation Study, "Performance Measurement Systems and How They Are Used As Employee Motivators," 7/1999, #07022. A summary was published in *APICS—The Performance Advantage*, February 1999, as a guest editorial by Gerhard Plenert. Additionally, more detail on the motivation-measurement relationship will be published in the *Production and Inventory Management Journal* later in 2000.

> **The measurement system directly affects employee performance.**

The author conducted surveys and interviews, and eventually experimented with a test case. He went to work for Precision Printers, Inc. (PPI), a company that was structured and focused on volume. Quality was treated as secondary in importance. It was not used as a measure of employee performance. A shift was made to eliminate the volume measure and focus on quality performance. The foundation of the belief was that, as in riding a bicycle, you first need to learn how to balance (quality); then you can learn to go faster (volume). However, the reverse is not true; going fast will not help you to learn balance. The transition from volume to quality occurred as a series of stages over about six months:

Production planning training.

Total Quality Management (TQM) training.

Goal/measurement system redesign.

Quality Week.

Team-based empowerment.

Ongoing continuous improvement programs.

The measurement transformation that occurred at PPI was to take the volume/revenue-based measurement system out. The company had built up one million dollars worth of unshipped customized finished goods inventory because the measurement system focused on revenue to be produced. If it was produced, it counted as manufactured revenue, even if it never shipped. The measurement transformation that took place changed the focus of the company to quality units produced. It was no longer advantageous to produce inventory. Inventory levels were limited to no more than 30 days.

The measurement change process started by implementing an extensive training program that focused on production/inventory management techniques. The training focused on how inventory buildup was destroying profitability. It showed that managing inventory was more important for profitability than managing labor. It also demonstrated that quality could improve only if it was measured and motivated by an incentive program. The current defect rate was costing the company money and chewed up valuable capacity. It taught the employees about how quality should be measured and that quality improvements come from the employees, not from management. Total Quality Management (TQM) training was also included. The TQM training focused on cross-functional team building with empowered ownership.

The next phase of the program required a point in time where the old measurement system was officially out and the new system was in place. This implementation point was set up as Quality Week. During this week the goal was to produce only perfect parts. The employees were given the freedom to tear anything apart, move anything, or team up with anyone. It didn't matter if only one part was produced, but that part had to be perfect.

Next, PPI had to reconstruct some new goals and objectives. Quality was the new goal and was defined as:

Defect rate reduction.

Customer complaint reduction.

Improved delivery performance.

Cycle time reduction.

Inventory level reduction.

All of these measures have a direct effect on profitability and customer satisfaction.

Quality Week began with a great deal of fear and trepidation. Management was concerned that the employees would just stand around, not knowing what to do. However, what happened was that most of the employees were excited. They had always wanted to have the time and freedom to attack the machinery and figure out why things happened and how they could be fixed. Teams formed spontaneously. Management basically had to get out of the way or else be run over. The employees were enjoying the experience, and several of them commented about how much fun they were having. The Quality Week program taught the employees about teaming, goal setting, and empowerment. At first some were skeptical, but once they saw the rewards for their performance, they became intensely involved in the process of improvement.

The total transformation from volume to quality took about eight months. The first three months were spent in preparation for the shift to quality (Quality Week), and the last five months were focused on the implementation of the transition. Some of the measurable results can be seen on the charts. Figure 9.1 shows how the defect rate was steadily increasing from May to October 1997. Then there was a shift, both in the direction of the trend and in the level of the defects. This chart demonstrates the most dramatic effect of the measurement change process.

Figure 9.2 records customer complaints and shows

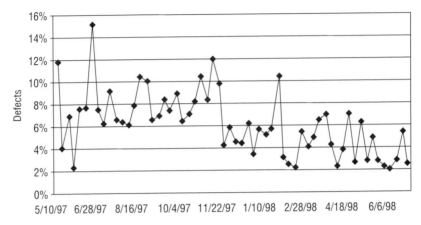

Figure 9.1   Defect Rates Chart.

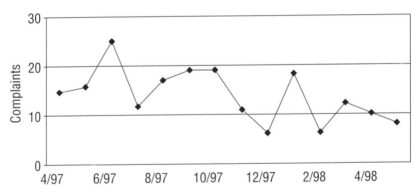

Figure 9.2   Customer Complaints Chart.

how they were decreasing because of the new emphasis on quality. Figure 9.3 shows that on-time shipment perfor-mance also improved in that there were fewer late ship-ments. This is directly related to Figure 9.4, which shows how quality improvements directly reduced cycle times. All these improvements are linked together, including the performance of the FGI (finished goods inventory) in Fig-

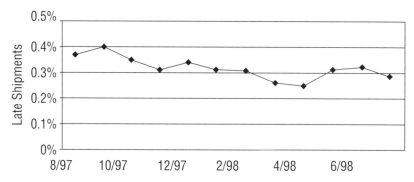

Figure 9.3   On-Time Shipments Chart.

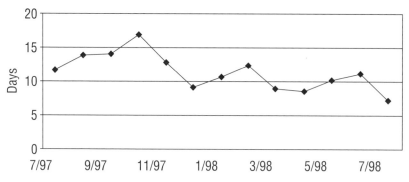

Figure 9.4   Cycle Time Chart.

ure 9.5, which has been steadily going down. Cycle time reductions reduced lead times, which made the organization more responsive to customer demands. Cycle time reductions also reduced on-time performance. And all these performance efficiencies were triggered by a measurement system modification.

Some nonmeasurable self-motivated results of the shift in measurement system to a quality measurement process include:

A strong shift from departmentalization to interdepartmental efforts.

Engineers working on the production floor.

Spontaneous teams organized to solve specific problems.

A shift in company culture to being "one big family."

Greatly improved communications.

Greatly improved customer relations.

This measurement-motivation research case example demonstrates how integrated their relationship is. Some additional findings of the overall research project (taken from the APICS Education and Research Foundation Working Paper) include:

First, corporate vision and mission statements (goals) tend to have very little to do with the measurement systems.

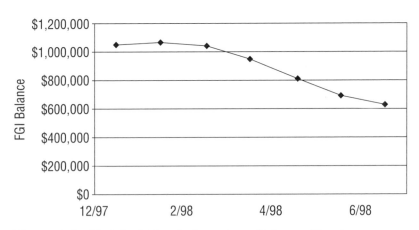

Figure 9.5   Finished Goods Inventory Balance Chart.

Tradition has more influence on the measurement methodologies than do goals. For example, a company has slogans and banners all over the facility promoting customer-oriented quality, but employees are still measured and paid incentive pay based on the number of units produced. These employees care very little about quality, since spending more time checking quality will directly reduce the amount of their paychecks.

Second, financial measures promote short-term thinking. Managers are numbers-focused and will do anything to make the numbers look good for the short term. Long-term investments are discouraged since they negatively affect the short-term numbers by increasing debt and costs. The result is that a "fix and patch" strategy wins out over a "replace with newer technology" strategy because it costs less for the short term.

Third, blanket corporate office–dictated international measurement systems don't reflect the local management style or culture and are often demotivating rather than motivating as desired.

Fourth, measurement systems are still thought of as data collection systems, and all data is considered to be a good thing. For example, after running statistical process control (SPC) for one year, one company contacted the author requesting some recommendations on what should be done with all the data. When the author told them to throw it out since SPC is a process tool for continuous improvement, not for data collection, they were very frustrated. Many companies have not yet realized that the measurement system is what directly motivates employee response, and that measuring the wrong things brings the wrong results.

Fifth, there seems to be no understanding of the relationship between goal achievement and resource efficiency.

For example, in most discrete manufacturing, labor is less than 10 percent of the value-added product content, and materials comprise over 50 percent. Yet, when cost-cutting measures are enacted, we still tend to focus more on the 10 percent and tend to ignore the 50+ percent. One company increased labor productivity by 10 percent (employee throughput) at the cost of decreased materials efficiency (lower inventory turns) by 5 percent (increased labor efficiency required more materials availability). Simple mathematics shows us that the increased labor efficiency increased profits by 1 percent overall (10 percent times 10 percent), and that decreased materials efficiency hurt profits by 2.5 percent overall (50 percent times 5 percent). Therefore, increased labor productivity cost the company a 1.5 percent reduction in overall profitability.

Now that we understand that a measurement system is critical to motivating the proper response from our employees, let's take a look at what measurement options exist in an FCS environment.

> Socrates told people what to do
> and they killed him for it.

MEASUREMENT

This chapter has been dedicated to a discussion of measurement simply because it's the most common area in which shop floor mistakes are made. For example, everyone has heard the story of the plant manager who attempted to follow "lean manufacturing" principles (run the plant with no wasted resources), only to approach getting fired because inventory reductions had destroyed his financial current ratios. The month following his chastisement, he repurchased the inventory. Similarly, there is the story of the plant that had one of the best quality systems available. It had statistical process control (SPC), total quality control (TQC), TQM, banners, Six Sigma programs, ISO certification, quality control (QC) circles, and more. However, the plant was being closed because of poor quality. The author was invited into the plant to discuss why quality was so poor in spite of all the installed systems. The answer was simple: The company was measuring performance and paying bonuses based on throughput through the work center. The evaluation systems stressed throughput, and, no matter how much hype was given to quality, throughput made the difference between getting fired and getting more pay. This brings us to an important measurement principle:

> **Increasing quality does not ensure increased competitiveness; it may decrease it!**
>
> **Increasing productivity does not guarantee increased profits; it may actually decrease profitability!**

Intuitively, this does not seem correct, because our training has taught us that increasing productivity and quality is a good thing. However, increasing productivity and quality in the wrong areas reduces the performance efficiency in other areas.[2] Let's take a look at some of the measures of performance that are available.

---

[2] Pieces of this section are taken from the book *Making Innovation Happen: Concept Management through Integration* by Gerhard Plenert and Shozo Hibino (Boca Raton, FL: St. Lucie Press, 1998).

221

Customer Quality

World-class customer satisfaction requires that the customer becomes central in the manufacturing planning and scheduling process. However, in order for customer quality to exist, it first needs to be redefined. Traditional definitions of quality revolve around the ISO definition of quality, which focuses on meeting or exceeding engineering standards. However, Japanese methodologies like Concept Management stress that a quality needs to be redefined as delighting a customer.

> **A delighted customer is one who is so excited by and attached to a product as to be automatically and unconsciously attracted to it.**
>
> **The excited customer is at the point where he or she will select a product based on emotion, and not simply based on logic.**

For customer quality to exist, we want to measure and motivate customer delight. To do this we need to interact with the customers and find out what delights them. The product team, responsible for a specific product, needs to find out what it is that generates this delight. Satisfaction is not sufficient. And the team also needs to realize that the target delight changes over time. It can't be discovered once and then be expected to remain the same. It is a constantly changing target.

An excellent book on quality is Ken Shelton's *In Search of Quality*, which lists the opinions of 43 industrial leaders on what quality should be, including the CEOs of world-class companies and quality leaders like Deming, Juran, and Crosby.[3]

---

[3] Shelton, Ken, *In Search of Quality: 4 Unique Perspectives, 43 Different Voices*, Provo, UT: Executive Excellence Publishing, 1995.

These statements should not be considered the last word on quality. Rather, they should be considered a benchmark we should all be ready to beat.

Productivity Thinking and Value-Added Thinking

Productivity has long been a measure of performance. However, traditional productivity measures in the United States have focused on labor productivity, ignoring other elements of the productivity equation. As already demonstrated, blindly focusing on labor productivity as a measure of success can result in a loss of profitability. Rather, what we need to focus on is "thinking productivity."

Do the Right Things before You Do Things Right.

Thinking productivity is where we look at the entire value-added content of the product and measure productivity based on the product's full content. Thinking productivity challenges the way we do things. It questions the purpose of all activities. For example, the purpose of data collection is not for cost accounting, but rather for motivation. If data collection is not generating the appropriate response from the factory and its resources, then it is a waste. All resources throughout the organization should receive a similar evaluation.

Benchmarking

Benchmarking is where we compare ourselves with others, both inside and outside of our industry sector. Benchmarking institutes exist throughout the world, tabulating and analyzing financial and operational data about companies and grouping this data into industrial sectors. For example, the American Productivity and Quality Group (APQG) in Houston, Texas, has a benchmarking institute that offers benchmarking services. Additionally, there are directories like Dun & Bradstreet's *Key Business Ratios*, which provides a published source for these ratios.

There are two types of benchmarking—internal benchmarking and external benchmarking. External benchmarking is where we compare ourselves with others that are in the same or similar industries. A key principle in external benchmarking is:

> As long as you're playing catch-up, the best you can ever get is caught up, and that's just not good enough.
>
> Or, stated in another way, copying your competitor won't help you beat your competitor. You need to think beyond your competitor.

If you're behind in the race, external benchmarking can be very valuable. But if you're trying to be leading edge, external benchmarking can cause complacency.

Internal benchmarking is where you compare your performance against yourself, either between departments, or the same department against itself over time. Internal benchmarking is a continuous improvement measurement tool that motivates change. It's the way the Japanese developed JIT over a 30-year period.

How Should We Measure?

Like all elements of an organization, measurement systems should be continuously receptive to change. We need to define, redefine, and re-redefine our measurement system as the organization changes. This includes a move toward an FCS environment. We need to focus the measurement system on the redefined organizational purpose. Additionally, we need to:

**Focus on the purpose of the numbers,
not on the numbers themselves!**

Conventional methods focus on measuring the speed of accomplishment. Rather, we should focus on the effectiveness of the accomplishment or on the long-term value of the accomplishment.

Resources flow toward what is measured.

—TOM TUTTLE

If we are measuring short-term improvements, our resources, including the human resource and its efforts, will focus on improvements in the short term. Therefore, if we want long-term improvements like customer quality, then we need long-term measures. In the United States the automotive industry has still not converted its plants to JIT production methods, even though experiments with plants like Saturn and Numi have been overwhelming operational success stories. This JIT transition hasn't occurred because everyone, from the CEO on down, is measured on short-term performance measures, and a conversion to JIT is an extremely long-term project. Who cares if it is beneficial to the consumer (higher levels of quality and lower costs of operation in JIT) or to the long-term stability and even existence of the company (vis-à-vis competition)? What's most important is that everyone, from the CEO on down, must satisfy the needs of the measurement system so that they can keep their job and get a raise. The same phenomenon exists for FCS. Organizations will resist moving to something that goes even beyond JIT, like FCS, because they fear that the short-term measures will be disappointing. The answer lies in reevaluating the goals of the organization to assure ourselves that we have a world-class focus of growth for our organization, as discussed in Chapter 8.

SUMMARY

A friend of mine has a son who was somewhat familiar with construction equipment, having spent a fair bit of time out on construction sites. Cement trucks have a beeper that goes off when they back up, to warn anyone behind them of potential danger. One day, while in line at a grocery store with his mom, he was standing behind a rather large lady wearing a beeper. Suddenly the beeper went off and the small boy excitedly yelled out, "Watch out! She's going to back up!" He was simply adapting a familiar measurement system to a new situation.

> **If you do what you always did,**
> **you get what you always got.**

Avoid getting caught in a rut of applying old measurement methods to our new FCS environment. This may result in a new system giving us old results. Rather, we need to reevaluate what it is that we are trying to accomplish. We need to look closely at our goals and consider what response it is that we are trying to motivate. And we need to consider the measurement options to make sure that the measure we select drives a successful FCS environment.

Chapter 10

FCS Success

*Leading edge world class principles teach us that the solution
to modern management problems is not found in identifying
their root cause, but in analyzing the purpose for addressing
the problem in the first place.*
—GERHARD PLENERT, *Making Innovation Happen:
Concept Management through Integration*

Gerhard's fifth-grade son, Zack, came to him with a problem
a couple of days ago. It went like this:

You have three boxes. One has two apples. One has two
oranges. And one box has one apple and one orange. Each
box is labeled wrong. How can you determine the contents of
all three boxes by removing just one item from just one of the
boxes? (See Appendix 10.1.)

This is a real "think out of the box" type of problem
that focuses you on the big picture. Finite Capacity Scheduling is also a tool that needs to be looked at from a big picture perspective. It is not a simplistic tool that is good for
everyone. Interestingly, however, the hospitals in Brisbane,
Australia, use it to manage their operations. And FCS

would be invaluable in solving maintenance problems like the space shuttle's low usage rate. Initially the space shuttle was slated to do one trip per week. Currently we get about six trips per year out of the three shuttles that are in operation. This is primarily due to the 90+ days that it takes to overhaul each shuttle after each trip. Limited resources combined with maintenance redundancies have created a tremendous backlog. FCS could be invaluable in this type of environment.

The purpose of this book has been to take manufacturing scheduling methodology into the future. The future requires us to focus on time. A futuristic competitive stance requires that we stay on the alert for techniques that will shorten cycle time, manage the supply chain, reduce costs, and increase responsiveness to customer requirements. Finite Capacity Scheduling (FCS) has become this tool of the future.

This book has exposed the inherent problems associated with infinite capacity scheduling and has pointed out the management changes required to move from infinite capacity to Finite Capacity Scheduling (FCS). This book has demonstrated:

➢ The production improvement potential available with FCS scheduling.

➢ How to be time-based and schedule for short cycle times and predictable due dates.

This book has taken the futuristic step of overcoming the long-term use of infinite capacity backward pass scheduling methods. It now requires management initiative to move forward with these changes. And the time to get started is *now!*

> **Even if you're moving in the right direction,**
> **if you're not moving fast enough,**
> **you'll get run over.**

The authors encourage your feedback, questions, and stories. Please contact them at:

Gerhard Plenert, PhD, CPIM
Senior Principal, American Management Systems
(AMS)
8545 Sunset Ave., Fair Oaks, CA 95628
Phone 916-536-9751, fax 916-536-9758, e-mail:
plenert@aol.com

Bill Kirchmier
Consultant on Finite Capacity Scheduling
Data Based Systems
P.O. Box 5031, Incline Village, NV 89450
Phone 702-833-3922, fax 702-833-3944, e-mail:
billk@databased.com

The Fifth Grade Problem

THE PROBLEM

You have three boxes. One has two apples. One has two oranges. And one box has one apple and one orange. Each box is labeled wrong. How can you determine the contents of all three boxes by removing just one item from just one of the boxes?

THE SOLUTION

The key to the problem is that each box is labeled wrong. Knowing that, if you take one item out of the box marked

Table 10.1   The Fifth-Grade Problem—Solution.

	Box 1	Box 2	Box 3
Actual contents	Two apples	Two oranges	One apple and one orange
Original labels	Two oranges	One apple and one orange	Two apples
Label change #1	One apple and one orange	Two oranges	Two apples
Label change #2	Two apples	Two oranges	One apple and one orange

"one apple and one orange," whichever item you take out of that box would identify it as the box having two of those items. Switch labels with the box that currently has the label you want. For example, if you pull one apple out of the box labeled "one apple and one orange" you would switch labels with the box that currently has the "two apples" label.

That leaves you with two boxes, one marked "one apple and one orange" and one labeled "two oranges." Since we know that the one marked "two oranges" has the wrong label on it, we know that we need to switch these remaining two labels. We now have the correct labels on all of the boxes.

Table 10.1 shows another example of the problem and its solution. In this case the item taken out of the box labeled "one apple and one orange" is an orange.

References

CHAPTER 1 WHY SCHEDULE?

Finite Capacity Scheduling

Kirchmier, Bill, "Selecting an Application: Finite Capacity Scheduling Methods," *APICS—The Performance Advantage*, Vol. 8, No. 8, Aug. 1998.

Production/Operations Management

Azadivar, Farhad, *Design and Engineering of Production Systems*, San Jose: Engineering Press, Inc., 1984.

Best, Tom, and Gerhard J. Plenert, "MRP, JIT, or OPT, What's Best?" *Production and Inventory Management*, Vol. 27, No. 2, 1986.

Johnson, Alicia, "MRP? MRPII? OPT? CIM? FMS? JIT? Is Any System Letter Perfect?" *Management Review*, Vol. 75, No. 9, 1986.

Pfeiffer, James, and Christopher Miller, "Viewpoint: Implementation Is Key to Becoming a World-Class Manufacturer," *Industry Week*, June 8, 1999.

Plenert, Gerhard, "Motivating World Class Performance," *APICS—The Performance Advantage*, Vol. 9, No. 2, Feb. 1999.

———, *Plant Operations Deskbook*, Homewood, IL: Business 1 Irwin, 1993.

Ptak, Carol, "MRP II, OPT, JIT, and CIM—Succession, Evolution, or Necessary Combination," *P&IMJ*, 2d Qtr., 1991.
Sarkis, "Production and Inventory Control Issues in Advanced Manufacturing Systems," *P&IMJ*, 1st Qtr., 1991.
Schroeder, Roger G., *Operations Management*, New York: McGraw-Hill, 1981.

MRP

Plossl, George W., *Manufacturing Control, The Last Frontier for Profits*, Reston Publishing, a Prentice Hall Company, 1973.
Plossl, George W., and Oliver W. Wight, *Production and Inventory Control*, Prentice Hall, 1967.
Wight, Oliver W., *Production and Inventory Management in the Computer Age*, Boston: CBI Publishing, 1974.

CHAPTER 2   TRADITIONAL SCHEDULING METHODS

OPT/TOC

Cox, James F., III, and Michael S. Spencer, *The Constraints Management Handbook*, Boca Raton, FL: St. Lucie Press, 1998.
Goldratt, Eliyahu M., *The Haystack Syndrome*, Croton-on-Hudson, NY: North River Press, Inc., 1990.
Goldratt, Eliyahu M. and Jeff Cox, *The Goal*, Croton-on-Hudson, NY: North River Press, Inc., 1986.
Goldratt, Eliyahu M., and Robert E. Fox, *The Race*, Croton-on-Hudson, NY: North River Press, Inc., 1986.
McMullen, Thomas B., Jr., *Introduction to the Theory of Constraints (TOC) Management System*, Boca Raton, FL: St. Lucie Press, 1998.
Plenert, Gerhard, "Optimizing Theory of Constraints When Multiple Constrained Resources Exist," *European Journal of Operations Research*, Vol. 70, Oct. 1993, pp. 126–133.
Plenert, Gerhard, and Terry Lee, "Optimizing Theory of Constraints When New Product Alternatives Exist," *Production*

and Inventory Management Journal, 1993, 3d Qtr., pp. 51–57. Reprinted in *Selected Readings in Constraints Management* published by APICS, 1996, pp. 23–30.

CHAPTER 3 CURRENT AND FUTURE SCHEDULING ADVANCES

Production/Operations Management

Azadivar, Farhad, *Design and Engineering of Production Systems*, San Jose: Engineering Press Inc., 1984.

Best, Tom, and Gerhard J. Plenert, "MRP, JIT, or OPT, What's Best?" *Production and Inventory Management*, Vol. 27, No. 2, 1986.

Brown, R.G., *Management Decisions for Production Operations*, Hinsdale, IL: Dryden Press, 1971.

Hadley, G., and T.M. Whitin, *Analysis of Inventory Systems*, Englewood Cliffs: Prentice-Hall, 1963.

Hanssmann, F., *Operations Research in Production and Inventory Control*, New York: Wiley, 1962.

Hax, Arnoldo C., and Dan Candea, *Production and Inventory Management*, Englewood Cliffs: Prentice-Hall, 1984.

Holt, C.C., F. Modigliani, J.F. Muth, and H.A. Simon, *Planning Production, Inventories, and Work Force*, Englewood Cliffs: Prentice-Hall, 1960.

Johnson, Alicia, "MRP? MRPII? OPT? CIM? FMS? JIT? Is Any System Letter Perfect?" *Management Review*, Vol. 75, No. 9, 1986.

Magee, J.F., and D.M. Boodman, *Production Planning and Inventory Control*, New York: McGraw-Hill, 1967.

Plenert, Gerhard, *Plant Operations Deskbook*, Homewood, IL: Business 1 Irwin, 1993.

Ptak, Carol, "MRP II, OPT, JIT, and CIM—Succession, Evolution, or Necessary Combination," *P&IMJ*, 2d Qtr., 1991.

Sarkis, "Production and Inventory Control Issues in Advanced Manufacturing Systems," *P&IMJ*, 1st Qtr., 1991.

Schroeder, Roger G., *Operations Management*, New York: McGraw-Hill, 1981.
Taylor, Frederick Winslow, *The Principles of Scientific Management*, New York: Norton, 1967.

OPT/TOC

See Chapter 2.

MRP

Plossl, George W., *Manufacturing Control, the Last Frontier for Profits*, Reston Publishing, a Prentice Hall Company, 1973.
Plossl, George W., and Oliver W. Wight, *Production and Inventory Control*, Prentice-Hall, 1967.
Wight, Oliver W., *Production and Inventory Management in the Computer Age*, Boston: CBI Publishing, 1974.

JIT

Karatsu, Hajime, *TQC Wisdom of Japan*, Cambridge, MA: Productivity Press, 1988.
Lu, David J., *Kanban Just-in-Time at Toyota*, Cambridge, MA: Productivity Press, 1988.
Miller, William B., and Viki L. Schenk, *All I Need to Know about Manufacturing I Learned in Joe's Garage*, Boise, ID: Bayrock Press, 1997.
Pascale, Richard Tanner, and Anthony G. Athos, *The Art of Japanese Management*, New York: Warner Books, 1981.
Plenert, Gerhard, "Line Balancing Techniques as Used for Just-in-Time (JIT) Product Line Optimization," *Production Planning and Control*, Vol. 8, No. 7, 1997, pp. 686–693.
―――, "An Overview of JIT," *International Journal of Advanced Manufacturing Technology*, Vol. 8, 1993, pp. 91–95.

————, "Three Different Concepts for JIT," *Production and Inventory Management Journal*, Vol. 31, No. 2, 2d Qtr., 1990.

Shingo, Shigeo, *Non-Stock Production: The Shingo System for Continuous Improvement*, Cambridge, MA: Productivity Press, 1988.

Chapter 5   Finite Capacity Scheduling

McNair, C.J., and Richard Vangermeersch, *Total Capacity Management*, Boca Raton, FL: St. Lucie Press, 1998.

Chapter 7   Finite Capacity Scheduling Implementation

Plenert, Gerhard, *The Plant Operations Handbook*, Homewood, IL: Business 1 Irwin, 1993.

————, *World Class Manager*, Rocklin, CA: Prima Publishing, 1995.

Chapter 8   The Role of Management

Plenert, Gerhard, *International Management and Production: Survival Techniques for Corporate America*, Blue Ridge Summit, PA: Tab Professional and Reference Books, 1990.

————, *The Plant Operations Handbook*, Homewood, IL: Business 1 Irwin, 1993.

————, *World Class Manager*, Rocklin, CA: Prima Publishing, 1995.

Plenert, Gerhard, and Shozo Hibino, *Making Innovation Happen: Concept Management through Integration*, Boca Raton, FL: St. Lucie Press, 1998.

CHAPTER 9   THE MEASUREMENT OF PERFORMANCE

Lockamy, Archie, III, and James F. Cox III, *Reengineering Performance Measurement*, Burr Ridge, IL: Irwin Professional Publishing, 1994.

Marsh & Meredith, "Changes in Performance Measures on the Factory Floor," *P&IMJ*, 1st Qtr., 1998, pp. 36–40.

News for a Change Staff, "Finding Your Way through Performance Measurement," *News for a Change*, July 1998, pp. 1, 4, 6.

Plenert, Gerhard, "Installing Successful Factories into Developing Countries," *International Executive*, Vol. 32, No. 2, Sept.–Oct. 1990, pp. 29–35.

———, "Leading Edge Production Planning Philosophies and Their Effects on Productivity and Quality," *Productivity and Quality Management Frontiers—V*, ISPQR, Feb. 1995, pp. 476–483.

———, *Plant Operations Deskbook*, Homewood, IL: Business 1 Irwin, 1993.

———, "Productivity and Quality in a Developing Country," *Productivity and Quality Management Frontiers—V*, ISPQR, Feb. 1995, pp. 194–202.

———, "Successful Factory Management Systems," *Produktiviti*, Bil. 42, Jul/Ogos 1992, pp. 2–6.

———, "What Manufacturing Resources Are Critical?" *Produktiviti*, Bil. 42, Jul/Ogos 1992, p. 14.

Index

241